INSIDE THE TAILHOOK SCANDAL

A Naval Avaitor's Story

Captain Robert L. Beck, U.S. Navy Retired

First Edition

Fulton Books, Inc.
Meadville, PA

Published by Fulton Books 2016

ISBN 978-1-63338-302-9 (hardcover)
ISBN 978-1-63338-303-6 (digital)

Printed in the United States of America

To my former squadron-mates

Rear Adm. Wilson F. Flagg, U.S. Navy Retired

DOD: September 11, 2001

Lt. Cdr. Barton S. Creed, U.S. Navy

MIA/PKIA: March 13, 1971

CONTENTS

Appendices

PROLOGUE

THIS BOOK WAS NEARLY TWENTY-FIVE years in the making. I began writing notes in October 1991 after I had gone to see my new Navy boss, Rear Adm. George Washington Davis IV, the Navy Inspector General. Thereafter, I saved official documents, newspaper articles, and scraps of paper on which I had scribbled notes and comments about events which were happening around me.

Eventually, in 1995, while still living in Annapolis, my girlfriend (now my wife), Stefanie, encouraged me to begin writing this story. About fifteen years before, I had met and helped Pulitzer Prize–winning author Seymour Hersh on one of his books, *The Target Is Destroyed*, about the Russian shoot down of Korean Air Lines Flight 007. I contacted him and asked for his advice. He recommended an associate who subsequently agreed to take on my project with me. Unfortunately, shortly after she began to review and organize my documents, she informed me that she was moving out of the DC area and would be returning all my material.

Since then, I continued to add documents to my Tailhook boxes, and in 2010, Stefanie and I became friends with Sylvette and Bill Davis, who live in our West Palm Beach condo building. Bill is a fascinating British raconteur who has had a very successful and wondrous life as an editor of *Punch* and writer, publisher, and commentator on radio and TV. After several conversations about my book-in-waiting, he refused to let the subject go, even writing me detailed letters about the book writing process. In March 2010, I finally relented and began, in earnest, to write this story which had begun in the autumn of 1991.

What was supposed to have been a four-day grand celebration of carrier-based Naval Aviation by naval aviators and naval flight officers in September 1991 certainly started out that way. Many of those pilots and crew members who attended this particular Tailhook symposium in Las Vegas, Nevada, had recently returned from flying dangerous combat missions against Saddam Hussein's mighty armed forces in the "Mother of All Battles." The younger JOs (junior officers), especially, were looking forward to the opportunity to party with their comrades in a city well-known for its over-the-top excesses and extravaganzas.

Some had flown combat missions from the flight decks of the USS *Eisenhower* and the USS *Independence*. These carriers along with their escorts had been dispatched to the Persian Gulf where they had taken up their assigned battle stations by August 8, 1990, as part of Operation Desert Shield, which was the United States' response to the Iraqi invasion of Kuwait just two days earlier. Others had been catapult launched off the decks of the USS *Midway*, USS *Saratoga*, USS *Ranger*, USS *America*, USS *John F. Kennedy*, and USS *Theodore Roosevelt* on thousands of dangerous and demanding sorties during Operation Desert Storm, which followed Desert Shield beginning in January 1991.

These returning warriors who were the very "tip of the spear" dimension of the fast attack carrier battle group would be joined in Vegas by hundreds of their brother "right stuff" aviators. Older and senior Tailhookers who had flown similar combat missions in every war and military action from World War II to Korea, Vietnam, and Iraq would also be in attendance.

This Tailhook tradition had been started by a handful of aviators who first met to celebrate their profession in 1956 in Rosarito Beach, Baja California, Republic of Mexico. In 1963, it was relocated to Las Vegas and quickly expanded exponentially into a full-fledged major convention attended by thousands of aviators, naval flight officers, aircraft and weapon manufacturers, industry vendors of all types, and many admirals who represented the senior hierarchy of Naval Aviation.

By all accounts, the Thirty-Fifth Annual Tailhook Symposium was arguably the all-time record setter. It is estimated that as many as five thousand people attended at least part of the four-day event, which included a wide variety of presentations that spanned the spectrum of Naval Aviation subjects. Discussion group meetings and the final event, the Admirals Forum, where the leaders of Naval Aviation answered questions from the audience, were standing-room-only events. The after-hours get-togethers at poolside and adjacent suites were also packed events. The concluding awards dinner on Saturday evening was a command performance.

The celebratory mood was, however, short lived. Just a few weeks later, events rapidly unfolded, which quickly led to a firestorm of criticism and finger-pointing of epic proportions. In aviators' language, it was a real "shit storm." Newspapers and TV, especially those inside the Washington beltway, were already reporting on the controversial Clarence Thomas-Anita Hill hearings, which primarily dealt with claims of sexual harassment. When, on October 15, the Senate narrowly approved Judge Thomas's confirmation by a slim majority, 52–48, there were many who thought there had been a grave injustice. Less than two weeks later, the TV and newspaper media picked up the Tailhook story, which to many seemed but a continuation of the Thomas-Hill issues and ran with it full speed. Almost immediately, there were universal demands that those responsible for the criminal actions be held accountable and punished accordingly.

The initial official Navy reaction to the stories of the wild behavior on the part of too many of the young JOs was to sever the relationship with the Tailhook Association. Additionally, two separate Navy investigations were begun, whose purposes and functions were neither thorough nor well-coordinated. In retrospect, it could easily be argued that the probability of success of these investigations was close to zero from the very start. And when their conclusions were finally reported after months of delay, they were seen by many as typical government "whitewashes" at best, or orchestrated "cover-ups" at worst. The truth of the matter is that they were neither.

Another even higher level investigation was then begun: this time conducted by the Department of Defense Inspector General (DoD IG), which only added to the perception that the Navy's two earlier attempts were seriously flawed. The DoD IG report led to further criticisms and even more finger-pointing both from inside and outside the Defense establishment. The Tailhook debacle had thus become a continuing major news story carried by all the major TV networks and the newspaper media.

Over the course of the three years following Tailhook '91, the various Navy and Department of Defense investigations resulted in lawsuits, courts-martial, and captains' and admirals' masts, which, in turn, lead to demotions, resignations, forced retirements, and firings that were both severe and widespread. Unfortunately, the consequences didn't end there. The ramifications have had lasting effects on Naval Aviation, the Navy, and all branches of the armed forces.

Indeed, even today, almost twenty-five years later, *Tailhook* has become a word inexorably linked to *scandal.* There has been a made-for-TV drama show, countless newspaper and magazine articles, books, and documentaries that have each addressed the various aspects of what constituted Tailhook and its aftermath. None, however, has addressed the many important issues that formed the backdrop of the actual processes, as well as the players involved. For instance, the internecine feuds among the various warfare branches within the Navy may very well have played a significant role in the investigations as well as their outcomes. Further, although some published accounts have been personal in nature, none provide the unique perspective of one who worked for both the accused and accusers.

What follows is the intimate story of Tailhook '91 written by a carrier-based naval aviator whose official positions before, during, and after the event provided him a unique and compelling perspective. Many of those whose careers were abruptly and arguably unjustly ended were his close friends, respected leaders, mentors, and heroes. Regrettably, one of the longest-lasting Tailhook legacies is that the US Navy and Naval Air in particular lost the benefit of the leadership of scores of naval officers whose outstanding careers totaled thousands of years of dedicated service. Not since the combat losses suffered during the eight-and-a-half-year air war in Vietnam had the Navy lost so many remarkable and patriotic aviators and heroes. The big difference is, at least then, they were doing what they loved!

Day of Reckoning

"Hey, Boss, they're out to nail you and all other Tailhookers."

I WAS IN A DAZE as I walked out of the building which housed the Navy's Office of Inspector General located in the Washington Navy Yard in the nation's capital. I kept repeating the same question in my mind: "How in God's name could all this be happening?"

After I had gotten into my car, I sat there for a few minutes as my mind raced back to several weeks before. I was thinking of my last official visit in late September 1991 to the office of the Vice Chief of Naval Operations (Air Warfare), Vice Adm. Dick Dunleavy—OP-05. He was the head of Naval Aviation whose office is on the "E" Ring of the Pentagon. The occasion of the meeting was my last day as the commanding officer (CO) of the Naval Reserve unit attached to OP-05.

I had been the unit's CO for the previous twenty-four months, during which time I had frequent interactions with the Air Boss* and his staff. On this last visit at the morning meeting of his senior

---

* The "boss" is a naval title normally used to describe the air operations officer aboard an aircraft carrier. He is responsible for all aircraft movements on and around the ship. The head of Naval Aviation is also referred to as the "boss" since he is, likewise, in charge all things aviation.

department heads, the Boss took time out to recognize and thank me publicly for leading my officers and petty officers in providing much-needed service to his office and the Navy. Ever the entertainer, he had everyone laughing as he described how amazed he was to see that I had performed my job well in spite of the fact that I was handicapped by being just a "Reserve" Navy captain. He joked that I had the additional burden of being an airline pilot who needed ten-thousand-foot runways in order to safely land airplanes. He ended his impromptu standup routine by wishing me well in my next assignment and career.

When the department head meeting was over, he invited me to remain there in his private office. He left me alone for a few minutes while he attended to some other matters. It gave me the opportunity to think how fortunate and lucky I had been to have worked for this incredibly talented and dedicated leader.

As I was admiring all the pictures and memorabilia on the walls and on his desk, my eyes focused on a picture of the USS *Coral Sea (CVA-43)*, an aircraft carrier which the admiral had once commanded. It was during that tour of duty as its commanding officer when I first met then Capt. Dick Dunleavy in 1980.

At that point in my Naval Reserve career, my rank was a Navy commander, and my position was the executive officer of VFP-206, a light photographic reconnaissance squadron composed of six RF-8G Photo Crusaders. The squadron was based at Naval Air Facility, Washington, DC, located on Andrews Air Force Base, Maryland. It consisted of ten officers and about ninety enlisted men. Along with seven other Naval Reserve squadrons, it was a component of Reserve Carrier Air Wing Twenty, CVWR-20, one of the two Naval Reserve carrier air wings.

Every year or so, the eight squadron pilots were required to requalify for shipboard air operations. For VFP-206, this meant that the pilots had to deploy aboard a US Navy carrier. On this occasion in 1980, the squadron pilots, along with the other F-4 Phantom II and A-7 Corsair II squadron pilots, would be practicing touch-and-go and arrested landings and catapult takeoffs aboard the USS *Coral Sea* while operating off the coast of southern California. Ordinarily, the entire shipboard evolution would normally take between two and four days to get all the pilots and crew members of all the squadrons requalified in carrier operations.

As the squadron's landing signal officer (LSO), I was required to be aboard the carrier for the entire duration because I was the one who "waved" (i.e., controlled the approach and landings of) the pilots in my squadron. Normally, unless I was either the controlling or backup LSO, there was little to do aboard ship. However, this shipboard period would be different because one of my best and longtime aviator friends was the executive officer of the *Coral Sea*—the number two man in charge—Capt. Jack Moriarty.

Capt. Jack and I had become friends while assigned to Attack Squadron 122 (VA-122) based in Lemoore, CA, in 1968. After completing the training syllabus for the Light Attack A-7 Corsair II, he and I were both assigned to Light Attack Squadron 113 (VA-113)—the "Stingers." Over the course of the next two years, we were first roommates aboard the USS *Saratoga (CVA-60)* for a seven-month Mediterranean cruise in 1969–1970. This was followed by a six-month stint back at our home base of Naval Air Station Lemoore, where the squadron transitioned from the A-7B to the A-7E: the newest and much-advanced and much-improved model of the Corsair II. In October 1970, the squadron then deployed aboard the USS *Ranger (CVA-61)* to West Pac and the Gulf of Tonkin to conduct air operations in the Vietnam War. There again, we were roommates for the duration of that cruise. Needless to say, the bonds of friendship, comrades-in-arms, and warriors were as tight between Jack and me as possible.

So, from the moment I found out that I would be reuniting with Jack, I looked forward with great anticipation to spending some quality time with my old roomie. Unfortunately, after arriving aboard, I quickly learned that his job as XO was as much an around-the-clock job as was his CO, Capt. Dunleavy. I only got to talk with Jack a few times a day for very brief periods. He was always being summoned to go off and see to something, fix something, or settle something. The one occasion when we did have time together was at a dinner where Jack and I were the guests of the CO in his private dining room. It was a wonderful affair where the conversations were interesting, fast-paced, and for the most part, humorous. It didn't take me long to understand why Jack had such high regard for his CO as Capt. Dunleavy was a remarkably gifted leader. His reward for his distinguished career to date was that he was made the commanding officer of a carrier. This was a Navy "first" because up to that point, only naval aviators (pilots) were given command of carriers. Dick Dunleavy was a designated naval flight officer who had served as a bombardier/navigator (B/N) in the A-6 Intruder aircraft. There was no question that he deserved his carrier command. Likewise, his performance as its CO would soon lead to promotions to higher ranks.

Now as the Boss walked back into his office, I rose and saw that he was all smiles. Handing me a cup of coffee, he asked me to take a seat on his couch. He began by reiterating how much he and his staff appreciated all the good work my men and women had provided his office. He remarked how seamless the process had been where one of my Naval Reservists filled in for days or weeks at a time for one of his active-duty officers during his or her absence.

We then discussed the recent Tailhook convention which we both had attended on September 5–9, 1991. Since the sixties, it had taken place in Las Vegas, Nevada. He wanted to know if I had anything else to add verbally to the written "after action" report I had given him a few weeks earlier. I told him that I had given that question a great deal of thought after I had written my report and unfortunately, I couldn't think of anything else to add. "As a celebration of Naval Air by naval aviators, it far exceeded any of the other Tailhooks I had attended. The professional symposiums as well as the presentations and the formal and informal social events and gatherings were all outstanding," I told him.

I think he might have thought that I was holding back something, so he asked me again if there weren't something that could have been added or done better. After thinking for a few seconds, I told him that "I missed the high jinx stuff which I had remembered from previous Tailhooks—like guys getting up on stage and joining the chorus lines." The Boss's response was that "behavior had gotten out of hand in the recent past, and so the word was put out to the junior officers, especially, to tone things down—a lot." My response was that I clearly could understand why changes had to have been made. "But still," I said, "I really did miss the high-spirited pranks which I had witnessed or in which I had participated in the past."

The honk of a nearby parked automobile jolted me back to reality. I spent a few additional moments sitting in my car recovering from my ordeal at the Inspector General's office and trying to decide what, if anything, I should do next. I drove out of the Navy Yard in search of the nearest public phone booth. I found one at a nearby gas station. I dialed the phone number of Adm. Dunleavy's office. His secretary answered. After we exchanged pleasantries, I told her that I had an urgent personal message for the Boss. She put me on hold, but shortly thereafter, the Boss came on the line and asked, "Hello, Bobby, what's so urgent?" I reminded him that I now worked for the Navy Inspector General as the commanding officer of the Reserve unit that supports the Navy IG—the same type relationship which had existed in OP-05 between him and me. As such, I told him, "Yesterday, after I heard and read about the Tailhook investigation underway at the IG, I called Adm. Davis and scheduled an appointment to see him this morning." I told Adm. Dunleavy that I spent about a half hour with Adm. Davis and then with two of his staff investigators—one civilian and one naval officer. He asked me how the meeting went. I took a deep breath, and as calmly as I could, I said, "Boss, they're out to nail you and all other Tailhookers!"

The Office Visit

"Isn't one admiral good enough?"

"WHY DO YOU SAY THAT?" the Boss asked. "Because," I said, "the half hour I spent with the IG and his staff and what they said and how they said it have convinced me that this is going to turn out badly for all of Naval Aviation." I then asked him how much he knew about the background of the Navy IG, Rear Adm. George W. Davis IV. He responded that he knew very little of the IG's personal history and career—but he did know that he was a submariner. I hesitated for a few seconds before I spoke.

Just a few hours before, I had made the morning commute from my Annapolis home to the Navy Yard in Washington, DC. The hour-long drive in rush hour gave me the opportunity to think about my scheduled office visit with my new reporting senior, Rear Adm. George W. Davis IV, the Navy Inspector General. I had only recently met him on the occasion of my assuming command of the Navy Inspector General's Naval Reserve unit in early October. This was an organization composed of thirty-five Navy Reserve officers and enlisted who worked part-time for the IG. After the half-hour-long change-of-command ceremony at which I actually assumed command, he spent some time with me welcoming me aboard his command and explaining to me all the benefits his office derived from the cadre of naval reservists who were now in my charge. He had made a very good impression on me especially by emphasizing his "open door" policy. I was now about to take advantage of that policy by meeting with him at his office.

I arrived at the Navy Yard and parked my car about a half hour before my scheduled appointment. I used the extra time to relax by having a cup of coffee at a nearby shop while putting the final touches on my imaginary speech to the IG. In my mind, I thought it would take about five minutes to explain all that I thought I had to say. I was feeling quite confident that it would be a productive meeting and a necessary one. Indeed, as soon as I had read in the recent newspaper that the Navy IG would be conducting an additional Tailhook investigation, I knew I was obligated to disclose the extent of my involvement to my new superior.

I walked into his office reception area a few minutes early where I introduced myself to his secretary. I only had to remain a minute or two before the admiral opened the door and welcomed me into his private office. He seated himself at his desk as I stood in my Navy captain's dress blue uniform at attention and told him how much I appreciated him taking the time to see me on such short notice. I then said, "Admiral, you are aware that prior to taking over my present Reserve unit here at IG a few weeks ago, I had worked for Vice Adm. Dunleavy at OP-05. I was there for two years as commanding officer of the reserve unit assigned to and working for OP-05. What I need to now tell you, because of your current investigation, is that I attended this recent Tailhook in Las Vegas. I was neither there on orders nor in any way as an official or in an official status. Further, I actually had a part in preparing for OP-05's participation at Tailhook." I was then about to go into the specifics of my attendance and involvement when the admiral stood up and started speaking, "You're telling me you attended this Tailhook in Las Vegas?"

"Yes, sir," I answered.

"So are you a Tailhooker?"

"Yes, sir, I am."

"What plane did you fly?"

"I flew the A-7 Corsair II from 1968–1973 while on active duty, and I flew the RF-8 Photo Crusader from 1977–1982 in the Reserves."

"Any combat?" he asked.

"Yes, sir. I had a nine-month combat cruise on the *Ranger* to West Pac in the Tonkin Gulf in 1970 to 1971. I flew 165 missions."

"Had you been to other Tailhooks?"

"Yes, sir, I've attended several. The most memorable was in 1971."

"Did you enjoy them?"

"Immensely, sir. They were fantastic. But this past one was probably the best."

Before I could say why I thought this to be the case, he began to speak to me in a far more serious and stern manner. "You know," he began, "you naval aviators have been getting away with murder all these years. Your behavior—not only at the Tailhook but frequently at your officers' clubs—is unseemly, atrocious, and certainly not acceptable as officer-like. I remember how humiliated I was as a teenager to have to drive the family car from our house to pick up my naval aviator father at the officers' club. He and his squadron mates would drink excessively at happy hour on Friday nights and other occasions. Then I would have to drive him home. I have heard all sorts of sordid naval aviator stories at Tailhook and other happy-hour celebrations throughout my career, and quite frankly, I am ashamed and disgusted by them."

There was a pause in his speech, and I was getting very uncomfortable. Before I could gather my thoughts and respond, he continued, "Well, Capt. Beck, naval aviators are about to be brought to judgment—finally. For far too long, you've been allowed to get away with unacceptable behavior. You're admired for your brashness and over-the-top stunts because you're perceived as heroes. That is about to change!"

Now, I was literally shaking.

"You Brown Shoes [naval slang for naval aviators] finally will receive your comeuppance, and it's not going to be pretty." He stopped speaking and sat down in his chair.

"I want you to go see one of my civilian Tailhook investigators and tell him about your attendance and involvement at Tailhook. Any questions?"

"No, sir," I answered and left his office and closed the door.

In the reception room, I asked the admiral's secretary to call my assigned investigator and see if I could be seen right away. After she hung up, she told me how to get to his office and that I was expected there in five minutes.

"Holy shit," I said to myself as I stopped by a nearby men's room to splash some cold water on my face. As I took a "nervous" pee, I thought about meeting my inquisitors. This was, in no way, how I envisioned my IG visit. The discussion had gone from calm to superheated in less than two minutes. I was upset that I didn't counter any of the IG's statements, but in truth, I realized that any comments made by me would not have solved anything. In fact, it was quite probable that anything I said would only have made matters worse. I smiled to myself recalling that "discretion, sometimes, is the better part of valor."

As I was directed into his office by his secretary, I saw that in addition to the civilian staff member, there was, as well, a uniformed Navy captain. After introductions, I was invited to sit down.

Both had pens and pads at the ready. They asked me to explain why I had requested this visit. I spent the next ten minutes explaining that I was the new CO of the Naval Reserve unit attached to the Navy IG, having recently taken over about three weeks before. I told them I had requested a private meeting with Adm. Davis and that I had just met with him and informed him that I had attended this year's Tailhook. Additionally, I told them that for the past two years, I had worked for Adm. Dunleavy at OP-05 as the CO of his Naval Reserve unit. I then went into some detail of what my role had been in planning for Adm. Dunleavy's participation at Tailhook.

After I had finished, the civilian asked me if I had attended the event in an official status. "No," I responded, "I was there quite like almost everyone else as just an attendee."

"When did you get there and where did you stay?" the Navy captain asked.

"I flew from Baltimore-Washington International Airport and arrived in Las Vegas on Friday morning and stayed at the Holiday Inn on Friday night."

"Why did you stay at the Holiday Inn instead of the Hilton like so many other aviators?" one of them asked.

"Because when I made a last-minute decision to go to Tailhook, there were no available rooms at the Hilton. Fortunately," I said, "I was able to find a room at the Holiday because that's where the crews from my airline stay during their layovers."

"So you fly for an airline?"

"Yes, I am a pilot at United."

The civilian inspector's next question surprised me. "Tell me where you were on Saturday night and what did you do?"

"I attended the formal awards dinner at the Hilton. Afterward, I socialized in the dining hall with some longtime friends of mine for a half hour or so. I then left the hall and changed clothes in a friend's room in the Hilton and took a cab to the airport. I then took a 'red-eye' back to BWI."

"So you weren't on the third floor at all on Saturday evening after the dinner?"

"No," I answered.

"You didn't even go to any of the third-floor suites?"

"No," I repeated, "as I just told you, I was never on the third floor at all on Saturday night." I could feel myself reacting negatively to their questions.

"Is there anyone who could substantiate the facts which you just described?"

"Yes, there are a number of people, some of them high-ranking officers, who witnessed my attendance at the formal dinner. However, there is only one person I know who actually witnessed my departure from the Hilton on Saturday night—Adm. Jack Moriarty."

"Only him?" asked the civilian official.

I snapped back at him. "Isn't one admiral good enough? Besides, I told you exactly what I did."

He responded, "One may not be enough. Can you provide proof that you took a 'red-eye' home?"

Because I had actually used my United Airline pilot jump seat privileges to fly from Vegas to BWI on another airline, I had not been issued a normal ticket, but I knew that I could, if I needed to, obtain written confirmation that I was on that particular flight. "Yes, I can. If there are no other questions, I think I'd like to leave."

The civilian inspector said there were no additional questions, but if there were, "How could you be reached?"

I answered that "my phone contact numbers are held by the IG's secretary as well as the Reserve liaison officer." I left the office with knots in my stomach.

The Boss startled me back into real time: "Are you still there?"

"Yes," I said. "Sorry. I don't know where to begin. Adm. Davis spent ten minutes verbally assaulting me for all the sins of Naval Aviation past. He described to me his humiliation at having to pick up his aviator father at o' clubs after happy hours. He's resented the hero status of aviators and abhors their juvenile and boastful behavior. I believe he's committed to punishing us for our sins." The Boss just listened as I continued. "After being lectured to by Adm. Davis, he sent me to two of his Tailhook investigators—one civilian, one Navy captain. I spent ten minutes with them. They seemed to be concerned only with whether I was on the third floor of the Hilton on Saturday night after the dinner event. When I told them I left the Hilton after the formal dinner and flew home to Baltimore-Washington International Airport on a 'red-eye,' their other concern was whether I could prove it."

The Boss thanked me for the "heads-up" call and for providing him my insight. He agreed that Naval Aviation would be facing some pretty stormy weather but that it would eventually get through it because it was made up of some of the finest officers ever to wear the Wings of Gold. I agreed with him and said, "You, Admiral, are at the very top of that list. God bless!"

3
Stingers Get an Award

"This is going to be fantastic."

AFTER I HUNG THE PHONE up, I got back in my car and headed home. The drive back in non-rush-hour conditions would be much less stressful: what was on my mind though more than made up for less traffic. In just a few minutes, I quickly crossed the Anacostia River and was heading north on 295. Before I knew it, I was on Route 50 East and had little to do with my mind other than just thinking about what just happened.

On one hand, the impression I had from my IG visit was that the equivalent of war was about to be waged against the Naval Aviation community. On the other hand, Admiral Dunleavy seemed to have taken my "news" in stride and had reacted far more calmly than I had expected. It dawned on me that maybe I had overreacted. While I was wondering what, if anything, I should do next, a Dean Martin song came on the "oldies" radio channel I frequently listened to. The song playing was "Everybody Loves Somebody Sometime," and I started accompanying the crooner whose TV show I used to regularly watch. My mind jumped from remembering one of Dean's funniest regular guests on his TV show to Tailhook '71 when many of us young naval aviators first saw, in person, Mr. Foster Brooks do his "act." Thinking of that Tailhook brought me back to remembering why I had attended that event.

Back in May 1971 after the combat portion of our cruise had ended, I had been one of the very fortunate ones to be able to get a seat on a "Magic Carpet" chartered Continental Airlines aircraft. These MAC flights carried military personnel who were under orders from Clark Air Force Base in the Philippines to Travis Air Force Base in sunny California. It was all pretty amazing how good my fortune was to be able to fly home in two days instead of having to spend almost three weeks aboard the *Ranger* as it sailed from the Subic Bay in the Philippines to Alameda Naval Station in San Francisco Bay, California.

Just forty-eight hours before boarding my flight home, I had flown my last combat mission as the wingman of our newly arrived executive officer, Commander Dick Grant. After a 5:00 PM launch from the deck of the *Ranger*, we rendezvoused overhead the ship in our A-7E Corsair IIs and proceeded northwesterly over the Gulf of Tonkin and eventually went "feet dry" over the coast of South Vietnam a few miles south of the demilitarized zone (DMZ) near Hue City. We flew west to Laos and proceeded north to the infamous Mugia Pass where we expected to meet up with a "Nail" forward air controller (FAC) and attack the targets he would assign us. All went well—just like the many other missions I had flown—to one of the most heavily defended areas along the so-called Ho Chi Minh Trail on the Laotian-North Vietnam border.

Once joined up overhead the target area with our FAC who was in his relatively slow-flying but highly maneuverable OV-10 Bronco, he proceeded to brief us with the required information about our targets which were trucks and suspected ammunition and fuel storage areas. He included as usual, where to "eject" if we were hit. Having received and "Rogered" his complete brief, the XO set up our bomb pattern and rolled in "hot" on the first target. I followed his pattern about fifteen seconds later. I was in my forty-five-degree bomb run at the same target when the area erupted after the XO's bombs exploded on the ground. I continued to press my attack and pulled up as four of my twelve 500 bombs left my aircraft. I flew back up to the medium altitude race track pattern (around sixteen thousand feet) preparing for my second run. I was surprised when I heard the XO's voice announce that he was "Winchester" (i.e., out of ammo) and asked if I had him in sight to join up and "bingo" (leave the area and head back to the ship). I told him he was in sight but that I still had enough bombs to make two or three more runs. The FAC then came up and said he had other targets nearby and asked would I stay around while he relocated them. "Affirm," I said. The XO added that we had fifteen minutes of "playtime." In short order, the FAC found more targets, briefed me, and I was soon in my second bombing run. This time, however, I could see muzzle flashes and see the not infrequent tracers coming my way. I dropped four more bombs off this time and went back up to altitude for my third and last run.

The FAC cleared me in, and this time, the "goomers" really opened up with their AAA. Their shell bursts and tracers were more numerous and much closer as I made my last dive bomb run. The four remaining bombs came off, as I called "clear." The XO had positioned his Corsair such that I easily visually acquired him as I was climbing back to altitude. He was heading south toward the DMZ. "Let's get the hell out of here," he said. The FAC thanked us for the good work. He said we got "multiple trucks and a few secondaries [secondary explosions]." He was aware that this was our last combat mission as the *Ranger* was leaving Yankee Station this very evening. We both wished him good luck and happy hunting and flew as fast as we could to get back to the ship to make the last Stinger landings of the cruise.

Meanwhile, the ship was heading into southeasterly winds, so it was actually heading in the direction of Subic Bay, the first stop on the way back home to the US. Because the XO and I were shot off toward the end of the final launch cycle coupled with the fact that our mission took us farther away than any other attack or fighter aircraft, we were the last two aircraft airborne except for the airborne tanker. The KA-3B "Skywarrior" tanker normally would remain airborne until all the fixed wing aircraft were safely aboard. After the tanker landed, the ship would then recover the last aircraft: the Life-Guard helicopter.

We checked in with the *Ranger*'s approach control about 150 miles from the ship after we had crossed the shoreline and were now "feet wet" back over the Gulf of Tonkin. The controller told us that we were in radar contact and that our signal was "buster"—go as fast as you can and get back to the boat ASAP. We immediately increased power and accelerated. We were instructed to execute a normal VFR day landing, which meant that you approached the ship from astern at one thousand feet and flew close by the ship on its starboard side. Once slightly past the ship, the pilot would then roll his aircraft into a forty-five- to sixty-degree bank turn to the left and perform a 180-degree change of direction. While rapidly decelerating from 350 knots to final approach speed of 135 knots, landing gear was lowered, flaps were extended, and tailhook was lowered. When the aircraft was about a mile and a quarter abeam the boat at 450 feet altitude, another 180-degree level turn was executed. Done correctly, the pilot would visually see and intercept the "meatball" (i.e., the light configuration that projected the proper glide slope) about a half mile from the stern of the ship. Once established on glide slope, the LSO would establish contact with the pilot and provide advice, if needed.

Generally speaking, the daytime landing procedure while demanding is kind of fun. You get to show all the many onlookers including all the off-duty pilots who are in their respective squadron ready rooms watching the TV that is broadcasting the live landings how good you are "around the boat." In the XO's and my case, however, it was no longer daylight. It was about forty minutes past sunset—no longer even a "pinkie." It was, as aviators say, a "no-shit night trap," but because it was the last recovery of the cruise with only three more planes to land, the *Ranger* was not using the nighttime landing procedures, which would have taken far more time.

At night or in bad weather conditions, an entirely different recovery and landing system was employed, involving procedures similar to operations used at the major US airports. Like all aircraft carriers, the *Ranger* had its own FAA-type radar room manned by Navy controllers. Each airborne aircraft is assigned a specific altitude and distance from the carrier to "marshal" (i.e., hold) and is given a designated time to depart the marshal pattern. When that moment arrives, the pilot exits the pattern and descends on his own heading toward the ship using his instruments while his progress is monitored by a radar controller. About ten miles aft of the ship, the controller begins giving heading and airspeed instructions. About four miles from the ship, the pilot begins descending from twelve hundred feet while the controller gives corrections to the proper glide slope and heading every three to five seconds. This continues until three quarters of a mile from the ship when the controller instructs the pilot to "call the ball." The pilot has meanwhile transitioned his visual scan from inside the cockpit only to outside. He keeps scanning his instrument panel, but more often, he includes the "meatball" and "line up" of the carrier deck in his scan. At this point, the pilot then calls the ball and flies his airplane, maintaining the proper glide slope and heading and speed. The LSO acknowledges to the pilot that he is now controlling and gives instructions, if required, to affect a safe landing.

Because we were using the daytime/good weather procedures, our landings were not just demanding—they would be very challenging.

Flying toward the ship in a standard wingman position, I was close to the XO's plane in "parade" position (i.e., about fifteen feet of wing overlap). After he executed his 180-degree left turn, I refocused my eyes on my instruments. After eight seconds elapsed, I too executed a sixty-degree bank level turn to the left pulling about three to four G's using the instruments more than usual because of the darkness. The XO successfully "trapped," and as he was taxing clear of the landing area, I made the normal radio transmission to the LSO: "Corsair Ball" for what I hoped would be my last approach and landing of this cruise. About fifteen seconds later, I was safely on deck, raising my tailhook, retracting the flaps, and folding my wings while carefully following the directions of the "yellow shirts" who were guiding me to my assigned parking spot. After my aircraft was chocked, my plane captain signaled me to "shut down." After I opened my canopy and while unstrapping, he climbed up the side stairs of my A-7 and welcomed me back and congratulated me for a good last landing. I shook his hand, thanking him for all his excellent work in making sure my aircraft was always "good to go."

I met the XO at Strike Ops where we debriefed the results of our mission to the air wing and staff "spooks" (i.e., the Navy intelligence officers). After that, we walked to our squadron ready room where we filled out our postflight maintenance forms and took off all our flight gear. Our own debrief was short and sweet—we shook hands and congratulated one another for successfully completing the last combat sorties of this cruise. As we were chatting and having a coke while we sat in our leather seats, the air wing LSO entered and asked us if we were the pilots in the last recovery. We told him we were, and he proceeded to debrief our carrier landings. This was an integral part of the shipboard life. Every carrier landing was graded by the controlling LSO and then debriefed during the face-to-face meeting shortly after the recovery ended. In this case, the LSO offered his congratulations and gave each of us an "OK #3 wire." This was the second highest grade a pilot could be awarded, and it was well received by each of us.

That evening after dinner, as was the custom, all squadron pilots and aircrews in the air wing attended the last "Fo'c'sle Follies" celebrating the completion of our last "on the line" period at Yankee Station. Humorous skits were performed by members of each squadron making fun of whomever or whatever would bring the most laughs. The vast majority of these very "colorful" skits, performed by the junior officers of the squadrons, always poked fun at the "Black Shoes" (i.e., the ship's officers) or the leadership of the air wing or individual squadrons.

After the show ended, individual squadron parties took place throughout the ship normally in a senior officer's stateroom or a junior officer's bunkroom or both. Technically, there was no alcohol allowed to be consumed aboard Navy ships at sea. However, each pilot was given a miniature bottle of brandy by the flight surgeon after each night carrier land to "sooth the nerves." The fact was that Courvoisier VSQ was not the drink most of us chose in order to wind down. Most, if not all, pilots and NFOs had their own "stash" that they had brought on board—and it was really inexpensive when purchased at the liquor store on base. A twelve-bottle case of Beefeater's Gin, Chivas Scotch, or just about any other hard liquor usually cost about $20 to $30. Needless to say, the supply always exceeded the demand. This last line party lasted until dawn.

The next day was a quiet day sailing back to the big US naval base at Subic Bay. Few organized or official activities took place except for the formal and informal squadron photo opportunities on the flight deck in front of a VA-113 Corsair—an event we all enjoyed. After dinner, smaller parties again took place. The one I attended was more like a family get-together than a celebration. I went back to my room early as I had to finish packing my bags for what I hoped would be my journey home the next day.

The ship docked early in the morning and by 10:00 AM I was off the ship heading over to the Operations Office at the Cubi Point Naval Air Station where I managed to book a seat on an Air Force helicopter heading over to Clark Air Base, which only took twenty minutes or so. As soon as I got out of the helo at Clark, I went directly to the passenger terminal with my orders in hand. My priority allowed me to get a seat on an all-coach version of a stretch Continental DC-8 that was scheduled to leave at 6:00 PM. Every seat was filled on the first leg from Clark to Hickam Air Base in Honolulu, Hawaii. After landing there, we cleared Customs, refueled, changed flight crews, and took off three hours after we landed. Next stop: Travis Air Force Base in northern California. We landed in midafternoon.

As I was trying to fly back to my parents' home in Dunedin, Florida, I tried to get on the first available flight to anywhere on the East Coast. It turned out to be on an Air Force C-141 cargo plane, which had about twenty passenger seats going nonstop to Charleston Air Base in South Carolina. We landed in the middle of the night and taxied to the Air Force ramp area. I was able to find a base taxi and was driven to the civilian side of the airport, where I purchased a ticket on the first early-morning flight to the Clearwater-St. Petersburg Airport in Florida. My parents were at the arrival gate to meet me, and then we drove home.

In less than a half hour, we arrived home, where I quickly unpacked my bag and took a long hot shower. In short order, I was relaxing, having my first beer with my parents and two younger brothers. It seemed almost unbelievable that just two days before, I was on the *Ranger* in Subic Bay, and two days before that, I was bombing North Vietnamese trucks and getting shot at while flying above the Ho Chi Minh Trail at Mugia Pass. Hard to believe—indeed!

The first few days of my two-week vacation leave were spent doing nothing more than chilling out. I would sleep in until late morning then have a late breakfast/early lunch with my mother in the bar area outside in the backyard. I would then relax on an inflatable raft in the small swimming pool. I had jury rigged the raft with a cup holder for the beer I was drinking while either watching TV or listening to music on a radio station. On the third or fourth day, my younger brother, Tom, had arranged a "hot date" for me. He lived nearby with his wife and son. As I was now ready to rejoin civilization, I had taken him up on his offer. That night, the four of us went out to party on Clearwater Beach. Around midnight, my brother and his wife called it a night since both of them worked and had to get up early. My date, fortunately, had no early plans, so we continued to party and wound up closing a few gin mills. I dropped her off at her home and drove back to my parents' home. As I entered the house, I was startled by the sight of my father watching the TV in the living room because normally my parents retire to bed around eleven or so. In rather a stern manner, he asked me, "Do you know what time it is?"

I looked at my watch and answered him, "It's three thirty. Is there a problem?"

He responded, "Yes, there is. Your mother and I were worried when you hadn't come home by midnight, and neither one of us could get to sleep wondering if you were in some sort of trouble."

Realizing that this is not the conversation I wanted to have, I said, "I'm sorry, Dad. Can we finish this discussion over breakfast in the morning?" He agreed, and we each went to bed.

I joined them at the breakfast table and with coffee in hand said, "I'm really sorry to have caused the two of you to have a sleepless night. I'm curious. Did you have many sleepless nights while I was on my nine-month cruise?"

My mom answered, "No, we seldom lost sleep worrying about you. I think it happened because you're now back in our house." I didn't want to cause them any angst, yet I did want to continue to go out and stay out late. I thought about offering to move into my younger brother's house for the remainder of my leave but knew that this would be a nonstarter for many reasons.

I then posed a question: "Suppose, from now on, if I told you how late I would be coming home at night, might that keep you from worrying about me?" They thought this might work and agreed to try it. That evening, after dinner and before heading out, I told them I'd be back by 2:00 AM. Even though I was having a great time, I cut short my date and returned home a few minutes before the appointed hour as I had promised. As I walked past my parents' closed bedroom door, I could see no lights on, so I assumed that they were asleep. The next day over a late-morning coffee with my mother at poolside, I asked her, "How did things go last night?"

She responded, "Your father and I had a good night's sleep. After you went out, we discussed the situation and realized that worrying about you just because you were home living with us didn't really make sense. We realize that while you were on cruise, you probably had been in far more dangerous situations when you were flying your combat missions in Vietnam. While we, of course, thought about what you were doing, we seldom lost any sleep."

I got up from my seat and went over to her and gave her a hug. "Thanks, Mom—it's really great to be home." With that, our worlds were at peace. *All's well that ends well,* I thought.

The remainder of my leave went by far too quickly but fortunately without any further parental issues. It had been just what the doctor ordered. Of course, my family and I were sad as we said our good-byes at the airport, but at least now, I would be talking to them by phone on a routine basis.

I flew back commercially to Fresno, California, where a friend picked me up and we drove the forty-five-minute trip back to NAS Lemoore, where I checked in to my new duty station—Attack

Squadron 122, which was the training squadron where pilots like me were taught how to fly the A-7E. I had requested this particular shore duty assignment months earlier when I had filled out my "dream sheet," which is the official document where you have the ability to prioritize your choices of future duty stations. I had submitted mine to BUPERS—the Navy's Department of Personnel from which all officer orders are originated. Because VA-122 had been my first choice, I was extremely happy to have received them during the *Ranger*'s last at sea period. I would become an instructor pilot as well as a training LSO. I was looking forward to these duties as well as getting qualified to pilot some other airplanes as well. I was in the midst of many new adventures when the *Ranger* arrived back to her home at Alameda Naval Station, California.

Along with some other "Stingers" who had also returned home early, we arranged to meet the ship with Welcome Home signs. Additionally, we helped the families of Stinger sailors in locating their husbands and fathers. It was good to see the ship again and be back aboard—if only to collect all my gear and personal belongings which I had left there. As soon as it was our squadron's turn to off load our gear, we got to work hauling our suitcases, boxes, and bags from the ship into a U-Haul truck which we had rented and then made the three-hour drive back to Naval Air Station Lemoore. A few hours after we arrived, the three of us had successfully transferred our belongings to our individual rooms in the bachelor officers quarters (BOQ) and celebrated with a few cold ones.

Weeks later in the middle of the summer, I was into my new job as an A-7E instructor and LSO in VA-122. It was a busy schedule of long days, but I was enjoying it immensely. One afternoon, I got a call from one of my former Stinger squadron mates who told me that VA-113 had just been named the first recipient of an award that Ling Tempco Vought (LTV), the manufacturer of the A-7, was sponsoring. It would be honoring the Stingers as the "Best A-7 Corsair II Squadron in the US Navy." It would be presented to the squadron at the formal awards dinner at the Tailhook convention in Las Vegas, Nevada, which was scheduled for September 10–12, 1971. Planning was underway to contact all former Stinger pilots who were on the

Ranger '70–'71 cruise and encourage them to sign up and attend. When asked if I thought I would be able to go, I answered, "Of course, count me in. I wouldn't miss it." I added, "This is going to be fantastic!"

Tailhook '91 Poster. Signed by designer, Hank Caruso. Inscription reads, "To Bob-love those high-speed pix, but where are they now?" He is referring to the photos I used to give him which were taken by the RF-8 Photo Crusader. (1991)

The author poses on a VA-113 Stinger, A-7E, Corsair II in his non-standard flight suit. The name of Jack Moriarty, the author's roommate, is painted on its side. (1971)

The author smiles as he "mans- up" his RF-8 for his final flight the day before he relinquishes command of his squadron, VFP-206. (1983)

The author, as controlling LSO, "waves" an RF-8 aboard USS *Saratoga* (CV-60). (1983)

Accompanied by the USS *Saratoga* Senior Catholic Chaplain, author has a private audience with Pope Paul VI in St. Peter's Basilica. (1970)

Author stands next to Capt. Jack Moriarty in his "Captain's Chair" on the bridge of the USS *John F. Kennedy* (CV-67). (1986)

The "150 Combat Mission Club". Ten VA-113 Stingers joined the club on their 1970-1971 cruise. From left to right: Lcdr. Jack Moriarty, Lcdr. Dave Pierce, Lt. Larry Hern, Lt. Denny McGinn (hiding), Lt. Rich Foreman, Lt. Rich Chapman, Lt. Al Klahr, author, Lt. John Rice. (Lt. Jack Waschbusch is AOL). (1971)

The VA-113 Stingers' "End of the Cruise Photo". (1971)

A VA-113 Stinger A-7E, Corsair II, on
a bombing mission. (1971)

The author in his RF-8 Crusader plugged in and receiving fuel from an KA-6 Intruder Tanker. (1983)

A pilot's view of a carrier landing aboard USS *Carl Vinson*, (CVN-70). 1982

The author, in his Great Lakes bi-plane, prepares to do a low flyby in the Severn River, Annapolis, Md. (1985)

Tailhook '71

"It is my pleasure to introduce the audience to Mr. Foster Brooks."

THE SWELTERING SUMMER DAYS FLYING out of NAS Lemoore located in the heart of the San Joaquin Valley were spent getting certified as an instructor pilot in the various phases of the A-7E pilot training syllabus. Familiarization phase qualification was followed by formation, navigation, weapons, tactics, and finally carrier qualification. Even though most newly arrived instructor pilots like myself had accumulated more than a thousand hours in the A-7 over the course of three or more years and had been carrier based for two or more sea cruises, it was necessary for all of us to learn a new skill set of how to teach the flight syllabus to new A-7 pilots. Additionally, I was spending as much free time as I could find in becoming qualified to fly the T-28B "Trojan"—a two-seat, single-engine propeller-driven trainer aircraft.

VA-122 owned about six of these aircraft and used them in a wide variety of missions. One of the most important roles was as a spin trainer. Because at the time all A-7s were single seat, it was far safer and economical to teach the new A-7 pilots how to recover from unusual flight attitudes, departures, stalls, and spins by putting them in the back seat of a T-28 with an instructor in the front seat. The flight characteristics of a T-28 were similar enough to those of the

A-7 that it was a quick and valuable learning experience consisting of one or two flights, which made the training very cost effective. The T-28 was also used as a spotter and safety plane for observing both day and night A-7 bombing hops. Additionally, it functioned as a sort of air taxi to pick up or deliver a passenger or parts to the myriad of air bases in California and adjacent states. Finally, and most importantly for me, the T-28 afforded a qualified pilot to use it as a cross-country airplane. This meant that I could get to various destinations on weekends far easier and much faster than by driving my car.

During this shore duty tour, I would also be pursuing my boyhood dream of becoming a member of the US Navy Flight Demonstration Team, the Blue Angels. Fortunately, during my *Ranger* cruise, I had met and become a friend and admirer of Commander Bill Wheat, who was the executive officer of our sister A-7 squadron, VA-25, the "Fist of the Fleet." Throughout the cruise, we had frequent interactions both professionally as pilots assigned to the same bombing missions and socially when on liberty during several in-port periods. Commander Wheat had been the leader of the Blues from January 1967 to December 1969. I had seen his team perform many times flying the F-11 Tiger and then the F-4 Phantom II.

Bill was an invaluable resource when it came to learning the inside scoop about the Blues, and during our cruise, we often had conversations about how best to pursue my goal. He told me that he'd introduce me to some of his Blue Angel friends after we returned home to Lemoore. One day in mid-July, I called him, and a few days later, he connected me to a friend of his who was currently Blue Angel #4, the slot pilot, Lt. Jim Maslowski.

The process to become a member of the Blues involved spending face time with all the members of the team at the various show sites where they performed. A few times later that summer, I was able to fly either an A-7 or T-28 to a naval air station and spend the weekend in their company. What a blast it was to hang out with them! Along with other Blue Angel applicants, I'd attend their preshow get-togethers, watch their performances, and then be an onlooker to their postshow celebrations. We'd dine with them and attend the hosted parties in the evening. It was even better than I had anticipated.

Before I knew it, the summer was over, and September and Tailhook were here already. I packed all the necessities and drove to Las Vegas alone in my Vette—my golf clubs occupied the passenger seat. The eight-hour journey began very early on Friday morning, and I arrived in the Nevada desert around noon. I checked into my room at the *Sahara Hotel*, changed into my pool attire, and headed down for some R&R.

The next three days were filled attending a few formal presentations and, of course, informal afternoon and after-hours parties along with the obligatory round of golf. Poolside at the Sahara was often the starting point for the evening's festivities. The atmosphere reminded me of spring break in Ft. Lauderdale or Daytona that I had attended many years earlier. Countless mini reunions and impromptu celebrations were the orders of the day. It was not unusual to venture out to other hotels and see familiar aviator faces all over Vegas—in the lounges, the game rooms, or at one of the many fabulous floor shows.

The highlight, of course, for us Stinger pilots was the formal awards dinner attended by more than two thousand aviators, dignitaries, and honored guests. The VA-113 pilots gathered beforehand for cocktails where we were introduced to the Ling Tempco Vought executives who would later present us the award which they were sponsoring. Also in attendance was the man whose name was now associated with the award—Rear Adm. Clarence Wade McCloskey Jr., USN (Ret.).

A few weeks earlier, we had received the news that LTV had named their "Best A-7 Attack Squadron" award the "Adm. McCloskey Award" to honor the man who holds a very special place in the history of Naval Aviation. In April 1942, LCDR McCloskey became the air group commander (CAG) aboard the USS *Enterprise (CV-6)*. During the Battle of Midway, he was leading his air group's scout bombers on June 4, 1942, in search of the Japanese carriers. It was his momentous decisions which ultimately led his *Enterprise* air wing in first finding and then destroying two Japanese aircraft carriers—*Koga* and *Akagi*.

Most Stingers were aware of Adm. McCloskey's iconic status before we met him at the predinner cocktail party, but it still was almost incomprehensible to actually be in the presence of the man who had achieved legendary status. All of us Stingers wanted to hear as many details of the historic carrier battles as possible from an eye-witness, and the admiral didn't disappoint us. Although he wanted to hear our stories, we managed to have him tell so many personal stories that his monologue continued throughout the cocktail party and through most of the dinner as well. We were all seated at one big Stinger table, so all of us took part in the dinner discussions.

However, all table conversations came to a temporary conclusion when the master of ceremony introduced the many dignitaries including two famous Air Force fighter pilots—Maj. Gen. "Chappie" James and Brig. Gen. Robin Olds. Earlier in the day, both officers had participated as principal speakers at the hour-long symposium discussion on the issue of the POWs in North Vietnam. Both men were well-known to the majority of the assembled Tailhookers. Gen. James reminded us of their time together when then Col. Olds was the commander of the Eight Tactical Fighter Wing, and he, Col. James, was his vice commander. They were based in Uborn Royal Thai Air Base, Thailand, flying the F-4C Phantom II in 1966. What many of us found particularly interesting was that it was during that time period when they were first referred to as "Blackman and Robin."

Both had remarkable careers. Gen. James graduated from the Tuskegee Institute in 1942 and began his military service as a Tuskegee airman. By 1944, he was an instructor pilot in the world famous all-Black Ninety-Ninth Pursuit Squadron flying the P-51 Mustang. In the Korean War, he flew 101 missions in the P-51 and the F-80 Shooting Star (Note: later in 1975, he became the nation's first African-American four-star general).

Gen. Olds, the son of a major general Air Force pilot, graduated from West Point in 1943. During WWII, he was credited with downing twelve German aircraft while flying first the P-38 Lightning and then the P-51. He missed out on combat during Korea but shot down four MiGs (two MiG-17s and two MiG-21s) in Vietnam where he flew 107 combat missions. His flamboyant style and signature handle-bar mustache endeared him to every US fighter pilot.

When the MC announced that the two legendary Air Force aviators were made honorary Tailhookers, the place went wild with loud hoorahs and thunderous applause.

A number of short speeches were delivered, the various awards were presented including the Adm. McCloskey Award to the Stingers, and then the honored guest was introduced: the head of Australian Naval Air had a distinguished physical appearance to match his impressive flying career credentials. His impeccable royal and aristocratic air highlighted by his trimmed white beard quickly got the attention of everyone, and soon there was silence in the dining room except for his baritone voice.

His speech about his flying career and the history of the Australian Naval Air was interesting but frequently interrupted by him pausing to drink from his nearby whiskey glass. A bartender was constantly refilling his glass from a liquor bottle. In short order, the admiral started to slur his words and increasingly used very "colorful" language. As his drinking became a major distraction, there were frequent belches, hiccups, and F-bomb utterances that all of us couldn't believe. Watching this spectacle, many of us went from being amazed to alarmed to feeling embarrassed to laughing uncontrollably.

Finally, the speech ended, and we were literally rolling in the aisles crying with laughter. Only after the admiral was poured back into his seat on the dais were we told by the MC that the "admiral" was actually the actor-comedian Mr. Foster Brooks who would soon become a regular "drinking" pal of Dean Martin on his weekly TV show. The masterful performance was award winning: Mr. Brooks had pulled the stunt off completely and convincingly. His act was the perfect ending to a memorable Tailhook. Afterward, many Stingers spent time socializing in the dining room and then accompanied Adm. McCloskey back to our party room on the third floor to continue to listen to his stories.

He revealed one unpublished detail of his famous flight which we found fascinating. On the way up to the flight deck on that fateful morning on the first day of the Battle of Midway, one of his squadron's senior enlisted tail gunners had fallen on a ladder (i.e., stairs) and had broken his leg. LCDR McCloskey and the plane's pilot had literally grabbed the first crewman they saw, put him in a flight suit, and strapped him into his aircraft as a substitute tail gunner. He was shown how to fire the machine gun, and off they went on their momentous flight. Adm. McCloskey told us all went well until after bombing the carriers. On the way back to *Enterprise*, all the returning planes were attacked by Japanese Zeros. The novice tail gunner had performed well except that he happened to have shot many of his own bullets into the rudder of his own aircraft while attempting to shoot down the Japanese fighters. The pilot could actually feel the bullets impacting the rudder but assumed that he was being hit by enemy fire. Not until after he successfully landed back aboard the *Enterprise* and was investigating the damage did he learn the facts about how the damage actually occurred.

All of us had a great laugh with that story and shared a few of our own. I related the story of one A-7 pilot who had returned to the *Ranger* one afternoon after a combat mission over Laos. He had a MK-82, a five-hundred-pound "dumb" bomb, still hung on one of his TERS (triple ejector rack), a weapon suspension unit that attaches to an aircraft's wing pylon. The bomb failed to release during his initial and subsequent attack runs. Later, he tried multiple tactics to get it to come off at a bomb drop zone in the gulf with no luck. I happened to be the controlling LSO when he landed back aboard. He flew an "OK" pass, but as his aircraft was rapidly decelerating after his hook had engaged the #2 wire, the bomb came off the TER and slid forward bouncing across the angle deck landing area and flew into the water ahead of the ship, thankfully, without detonating. As it was shooting over the deck, the pilot announced Winchester (i.e., out of ammo). All of us who witnessed the landing and heard the transmission agreed that it was one of the coolest spontaneous transmissions we had ever heard. The pilot was my friend Commander Bill Wheat!

It was also an incredible coincidence that one of our Stinger pilots, LCDR Bill Leslie, had a great deal in common with Adm.

McCloskey. Bill's father was Max Leslie, who was also a naval aviator and like McCloskey, had a prominent role in the Battle of Midway.

At about the same time that LCDR McCloskey was leading his Scouting Six and Bombing Six Squadrons from *Enterprise* in destroying two Japanese fleet carriers, LCDR Leslie, the CO of the USS *Yorktown*'s *(CV-5)* Bombing Three, was leading his squadron's attack on another Japanese carrier *Soryu*. She was so severely damaged by the bombs dropped by his squadron's planes that she too sunk later that evening of June 4, 1942.

It was a once-in-a-lifetime occurrence where we Stingers were firsthand witnesses to the stories of two famous naval aviators who were pivotal players in what most historians believe to have been the greatest modern-day naval battle. And yet the reality was that it would be years before the aviators from *Enterprise* and *Yorktown* would receive the recognition they so richly deserved. When questioned about this controversy of who exactly got the credit for the destruction of the four Japanese aircraft carriers, Adm. McCloskey told us at the time it was clear to everyone in the Navy chain of command in the battle group that it was the dive-bombing Dauntless pilots who were responsible. Indeed, the after action reports from the Navy task force commanders leave no doubt as to whose bombs destroyed which ships. And yet, for a variety of reasons, the story which most US citizens received at the time was dramatically different.

Many news stories published throughout the country shortly after the battle painted the picture that the Army Air Force (AAF)—most especially the B-17 crews—flying out of the base on Midway were responsible for the destruction of the Japanese fleet. How and why this occurred has since been a subject encompassing volumes of analyses.

Beginning on June 3, 1942, many sorties were flown by aviators from the airfield on Midway. There were sixteen AAF B-17 Flying Fortresses who flew high-altitude-level bombing missions against the enemy fleet as well as four torpedo-equipped B-26 Marauders. There were also Navy and Marine Corps pilots flying six TBF Avengers, four Vought SB2U Vindicators, and sixteen SBD Dauntlesses. While the Army Air Corps accounted for more than fifty sorties dropping more than ninety-two tons of ordnance, the Navy and Marine pilots dropped an additional twenty-five tons.

The source of those initial post battle news reports was the AAF B-17 crews who had subsequently returned to Hawaii. "Army fliers blasted two fleets at Midway—big bombers won" was the *New York Times* headline of June 11, 1942, and is but one of many examples of the AAF being the first to get to the media and thus have their story told to the public. Another similar headline appeared about the same time: "How Army Air Corps won Battle of Midway—pilots deliver first news; every bomb sinks a ship."

For years after the actual battle, the Navy allowed the story to go on without challenging its veracity or refuting it with its own factual data. There were many reasons why it took so long for the facts to emerge, but they can be summarized in two words: secrecy and censorship. To have released details of the real story would have necessarily provided information about the US Navy fleet that was highly classified—for good reasons. Additionally, the Navy brass wasn't willing either to engage in interservice rivalry or to publicly contradict statements made by administration officials including the secretary of war. Even as late as April 1944, Adm. King, the commander in chief of the United States Fleet and chief of Naval Operations, in a comprehensive report to the secretary of the Navy, attributed the destruction of the Japanese fleet to the Midway-based AAF planes and their crews.

Eventually after the war ended, the true story was publicized. While the AAF, Navy, and Marine Corps pilots flying from Midway deserve great credit for their heroic attacks against the enemy, there is no doubt that not a single bomb or torpedo of theirs found its target and thus did no damage. What they did do, however, especially the brave crews of the torpedo-laden B-26s, was to engage the enemy at a critical time, which significantly disrupted their invasion plans and order of battle. This disruption allowed the subsequent attack by the carrier-based pilots to be as effective as it was. The most incredible fact remains: in less than a ten-minute period around 10:30 AM on Monday, June 4, 1942, the dive-bombing Dauntless pilots from *Enterprise* and *Yorktown* set ablaze three enemy carriers which eventually sunk. Still later that same day, Dauntless aviators from both carriers flying from the *Enterprise* destroyed the fourth and last remaining Japanese carrier.

Having discussed most of this story with Adm. McCloskey that evening, I remember his concluding remark with which I had previously become familiar: "He who gets back to the ready room first to tell his story wins the air-to-air engagement." Again, we shared a good laugh realizing that some things never change!

My journey down Tailhook memory lane ended as I left Route 50 at the Rowe Blvd exit. Driving past the Navy-Marine Corps Stadium, I quickly navigated around Church Circle, went down Duke of Glouster St. and over the draw bridge into Eastport. A few minutes later, I was in my townhouse home in Chesapeake Landing, changing into my workout clothes. As the midafternoon weather was perfect for outdoor activity, I decided to go on a bike ride through Quiet Waters Park and then on to the Bay Ridge and Highland Beach area southeast of Annapolis situated along the Chesapeake Bay shoreline. One of the great joys of living here was to be able to experience the incredible sights and sounds associated with one of the most beautiful bodies of water in the US. Few places offer as tranquil and serene settings as I experienced on my frequently traveled bike route. It was both a rewarding and exhilarating three-hour afternoon excursion.

It was often part of my after-workout routine to grab a cold beer from my frig and walk the seventy-five yards down to the dock at Chesapeake Landing. Not only was there an unobstructed view south and east to the bay but also north to the Naval Academy and Severn River. I never tired of seeing the Naval Academy sailboats of all types, YPs (Yard Patrol Craft) and all the other pleasure and commercial vessels that are always present. This particular afternoon, I watched as a skipjack made her return from the bay to the city dock. As her crew deployed her push boat and furled her majestic mainsail, I thought about the several times I had crewed on the *Anna McGarvey*, a skipjack built for and owned by my close friend, Michael Ashford. Over the previous thirteen years whenever I had a difficult experience similar to the one I had today which I needed to share, Mike was my sounding board.

As soon as I returned from the dock, I phoned him to see if he were available for dinner and a debrief/counseling session. I reached him at his Annapolis home and told him that I had an interesting story to tell him. "Can we meet later for dinner?"

"Of course, Bobby. See you around seven thirty."

"Thanks, Mike. See you later."

There was no reason to discuss where we would meet: it would be at Manus McGarvey's Waterfront Saloon and Oyster Bar in downtown Annapolis—an establishment built and owned by Mike since 1975. For a large number of aviators, sailors, and a wide variety of fun-loving people, Mike's saloon was our Annapolis Cheers—"a place where everybody knows your name."

The 912 Annapolis Gang

"A very big story for a very long time."

October nights in Annapolis arguably have the best weather conditions of the year. The clear, cool autumn air is devoid of the excessive humidity of the summer months and produces fabulous evenings. Because it was just such a night, I decided to make the short two-mile drive downtown on my Harley Low Rider. Taking my bike had the advantages of providing natural air-conditioning and more importantly finding a desirable parking spot. Even during the week, locating an open parking space for a car was problematic at best, but there were always vacant motor cycle spaces close by the saloon.

As I walked through the front entrance swinging doors shortly before 7:30 PM, I was welcomed by one of the assistant managers who asked if I would be dinning and did I need a table. "I'll be having dinner with the Captain, and I'm pretty sure we'll want to be in the Aviator Room. I take it he hasn't arrived yet?"

"No, Bob. But I'll tell him you're here when he arrives." With that, I said "Hi" to one of my favorite bartenders, Guido, whom I'd known since he first began working here many years ago—he, too, is an ardent Yankee fan. I gave him a thumbs-up as he pointed to the Aviator beer tap. Years before, Mike and a group of his drinking buddies including me had helped design this particular draft beer, which was brewed exclusively for McGarvey's Saloon. It had soon became very popular among the regular clients. In addition to the beer, Mike had also designed its logo, which featured a Waco biplane and a World War I aviator decked out in his flying leathers, goggles, and helmet. Mike's and my old boss at Easter Air Lines, Capt. Eddie Rickenbacker, would have loved the character and symbolisms.

As I took my first gulp, I heard someone call my name. I looked over to the front corner of the bar and saw a few of my friends looking at me. "Come on over and join us, Bobby." I did and was soon surrounded by a bunch of my fellow Annapolitans who, like me, spent many nights socializing in the saloon. The group gathered here that night was typical of the McGarvey's crowd: it included airline pilots and flight attendants, doctors and nurses, attorneys, accountants, bankers, real estate agents and developers, writers, entrepreneurs, and other professionals. What they all shared in common was either a love of boating, flying, enjoying good company and varied conversations, or just having fun with good-natured friends. The mood was always lighthearted, quick witted, and jovial.

Mike had spent over sixteen years running his favorite watering hole, and its character was a direct reflection of his charm and personality. He had mastered the art of being a successful saloon keeper and restaurateur by thoroughly immersing himself in all matters. He had personally designed and created every detail of his place and its furnishings and never skimped in the process. His employees were superb. They were gregarious, good-natured, fun loving, friendly, and extremely loyal—in other words, they were just like their boss.

It wasn't long before I saw Mike enter his saloon where he was immediately cornered by some of his pals. For the next fifteen minutes or so, he worked his way down the long bar talking with almost everyone seated or standing. He then made his way back stopping at each table to greet his friends and guests. He finally made it to the corner of the bar where I was standing.

"Hi, Mike. Looks like another great night at the saloon. How's it going?"

"Fine, Bobby. It does look like it could be another late night for the Captain. Did you fly today and is that what you wanted to discuss?"

"No, I had today off, but I do have an early-morning getup tomorrow for a turnaround out of Dulles, so it will be an early night for me, at least. Sorry, tonight I won't be your late-night wingman. I actually spent the day doing Navy stuff—that's what I wanted to discuss with you, but I'm also famished. Can we have dinner in the Aviator Room, I'm pretty sure it's open?"

"Sure. Why don't you go back there? I need to have a short meeting with Jimmy—I'll join you in a minute."

As Mike walked off in search of his manager, I said good-bye to my friends and headed back to the semiprivate Aviator Room. The table there could accommodate up to ten patrons, but it had been set up for just the two of us. One of my favorite waiters, Bobby, came over soon after I sat down. I told him that the captain would be joining me momentarily and asked if he would bring me a "Fred Special"—a local cocktail designed by and named for Fred Celce, one of our gang of aviators. Mike arrived just as Bobby came back with my drink. We toasted each other's good health, and I asked Mike how he had spent his day. He told me he had gone over to the Easton Airport and had a wonderful hour-long flight in his Waco biplane.

Bobby came back to take our dinner orders. While Mike ordered the fish of the day, Bobby asked if I'd have my usual—a medium-rare bacon cheddar cheese burger and a baked potato. "Perfect, thanks," I said.

"So tell me what happened today in the Navy?"

It took me about fifteen minutes to describe my Navy IG visit and subsequent phone conversation with Adm. Dunleavy. "Geez, you had quite the Navy day, didn't you?" said Mike. He, like so many of my ex-military airline pilot Annapolis buddies, had been closely following the almost daily Tailhook news stories appearing in the papers and on TV. Additionally, Mike had met and in some cases had become a close friend of several of the people whose names were frequently mentioned in these Tailhook stories.

"So I take it you think that this will be a big story for quite a while?"

"No doubt about it," I said. "As much as I'd like to believe that this will only be a short story soon forgotten by the press, my gut tells me otherwise. From my experience today combined with recent headlines, I think this is going to be a very big story for a very long time."

"What do you make of Adm. Dunleavy's reaction to what you had told him about the IG and his investigation? If I were in his shoes, I'd be very wary that the IG's personal biases against the aviation community would unduly and unfairly hinder the investigation," Mike said.

As he was talking, I was reminded that I had introduced Mike to Adm. Dunleavy in the summer of 1986 on the occasion of the reopening of the Statue of Liberty on July 4. During the week of that celebration, there gathered in New York Harbor a massive array of ships from all over the world. Many countries had sent their Tall Ships to take part in the Naval Review. There was also a flotilla of modern-day warships including both the United States battleship USS *Iowa* and the carrier USS *John F. Kennedy*. Mike and his wife, Carol, attended the festivities as guests of Secretary of the Navy and Mrs. John F. Lehman.

As my ex-Stinger roommate, Capt. Jack Moriarty, was the commanding officer of the *Kennedy*, he had invited me and a group of my Annapolis friends whom he had previously gotten to know to be his guests as well. When the entire gang including Mike and Carol were aboard the *Kennedy* for an early-afternoon event, I had the occasion to personally introduce everyone to Adm. Dunleavy, who was then a vice admiral whose position was commander, Carrier Group FOUR/commander, Striking Force Atlantic. All were tremendously impressed by the admiral and the captain—not just because of their professionalism but also because of their friendly demeanor and welcoming good nature.

"He's certainly come a long way since you first met him in '86 in NY Harbor aboard the *Kennedy*, but he hasn't really changed at all. In fact, I'm still amazed that he was as calm as he seemed to be after

I delivered the bad news. The only thing I know for certain is that he will always do the right thing—no matter the consequences. I'm also convinced that lots of heads will roll before all this is over—and many of them will have had nothing to do with the Paula Coughlin gauntlet business."

After dinner, I joined Mike in the oyster bar section for "one for the ditch." It was apparent to both of us that the gang who were now in the saloon would make it a late night for Mike—and me, if I stayed. In spite of my wanting to participate, discretion took over, and I offered my regrets to Mike that I would be leaving soon.

I did, however, offer to help him find a suitable wingman in my absence. As usual, Mike, was not very receptive to the news of my departure, but eventually he eased off. While he was chatting with some friends, I conveniently slipped out unnoticed by Mike who was now a fully engaged fighter pilot.

The next day, I flew as a second officer (flight engineer) on a United 727 on a turnaround from Dulles to San Juan, Puerto Rico, and then a return flight back to Dulles. They were both very relaxing flights—a great crew of pilots and flight attendants, beautiful weather, and on time. The seven uneventful hours of flight time gave me the opportunity to reflect on the previous day's revelations. As I was driving home from Dulles, I wondered what reactions my other Annapolis buddies would have after I told them about my Navy IG visit.

I soon learned that I wouldn't have to wait to call any of them after I got home because there were several messages on my phone answering machine. It seems that Mike had already briefed a bunch of them at our daily breakfast hang out: *Jim's Corner*—home of the 912th Aero Squadron. They had spread the word to other members of our group, and all were counting on me to fill in the details at tomorrow morning's breakfast get-together at Jim's.

I woke up earlier than I planned at 6:15 AM and decided to put the extra time before breakfast to good use—play a fast round of golf at the nearby golf course at the Naval Academy. I quickly suited up, grabbed my clubs, and drove the fifteen-minute route through

Annapolis, past the Academy grounds over the Severn River Bridge to the course.

Upon arriving at the parking lot, I was glad to see that none of the other early sign ups had arrived. I quickly put on my golf shoes, threw my bag on my back, and walked the fifty yards to the first tee. I stretched for a few minutes then swung a couple of clubs for a few minutes then took my driver and successfully teed off hitting my golf ball in the fairway. For the next two hours and fifteen minutes, I thoroughly enjoyed my good walk over the eighteen holes. Although I would much rather play as a member of a foursome, or a twosome, I try not to miss any opportunity to get a round in. Except for seeing an occasional four-legged animal, I seemed to be alone. After finishing the round, I loaded my clubs into my car, changed shoes, and headed back to Jim's Corner, arriving there a few minutes after 9:00 AM.

Back in the late '70s, a few of my airline pilot pals had begun searching for a suitable meeting place for breakfast at various locations in and around Annapolis. What they had hoped to find was an early morning equivalent of our evening gathering place, McGarvey's. We eventually found everything we wished for at Jim's Corner. It was an old-fashion lunch counter/dinette with several tables—total capacity of about twenty-five people. Locals frequented the place both for breakfast and lunch. Its owner and cook was Bill Alexopolous, a WWII B-25 crew member—his wife, Liz, was the waitress. Over the years, every morning, there were between two and twelve of us who would meet for breakfast. The place eventually became known as Jim's Corner—home of the 912th Aero Squadron, since our unofficial meeting time was 9:12 AM, a tradition initiated by two TWA pilots in our gang: Peter Nevins and Fred Celce.

To Bill and Liz, we became part of their family, and we selected Bill to be the squadron's honorary commanding officer. Throughout the years, it served as our unofficial "ready room" and "mess hall," which we decorated appropriately. There were airplane models, Navy and Air Force logos, pictures, and all sorts of flying memorabilia. In fact, the latest addition to the collection was a poster of the "Dream Girls of Las Vegas," which I had brought back from Tailhook '91. I framed it and presented it at a small ceremony to Bill, who promptly hung it up on one of the walls. When I next saw it at a breakfast several days after the ceremony, I was upset that someone (I correctly surmised that it was Liz) had scotch taped tiny pieces of paper in strategically located places on the girls' bodies in the picture to more fully "clothe" them. I later found out from Bill that it was either let Liz do her cover-up fix or take down the three-by-two-foot poster entirely. I agreed that he chose the better option.

I parked my car in the adjacent lot and walked through the back entrance to the room. I paused at the counter to say "Hello" to Bill and grab my personal NY Yankee coffee mug. I was glad to see that most of my flyboy buddies were already seated and having coffee. Two tables had been joined together so the nine of us could easily and comfortably be seated. As I took my seat, we all exchanged our good mornings. As we were chatting, Liz came over and took our orders. After she had left, my friend, Luke, asked me to fill everyone in on my latest Tailhook episode. I told them essentially what I had told Mike two nights before. Unfortunately for Mike who was present, he was witnessing a repeat performance. Since the group this morning consisted exclusively of airline pilots who were all either ex-naval or ex-air force or ex-army aviators, it was a typical shorthand pilot brief of the facts: Fred Celce (ex-Air Force), Luke Colbert (ex-Air Force), and Pete Nivens (ex-Navy) were all TWA pilots; Bill Brown (ex-Air Force), Bob Eaves (ex-Navy), and Tim Martin (ex-Army) were American pilots; Mike Ashford (ex-Air Force) and John Ashmore (ex-Navy) had been Eastern pilots with me—John had since become a US Air pilot.

The discussion which followed was lively and thoughtful but frequently punctuated with references to the "good old days" and laments of "what's next." Since all of the group had known of and become acquainted with Adm. Dunleavy, some of the talk had been concerned with the effects on him personally and on Naval Aviation in general. Since all of us had a military background, I think, to a man, we realized the grim realities of what would, no doubt, be a long, laborious, and punishing front-page assault on our previous profession.

The morning get-together lasted until 11:00 AM when we were all paying our bills and saying our good-byes. As I was leaving, I happened to glance up and saw the Dream Girls poster and chuckled at Liz's modifications which solved her problem. I hoped there could be found such a simple solution to the Naval Aviation Tailhook problem but knew, unfortunately, that this were but wishful thinking on my part.

The Admiral and His Aide

"His apparent failure to take timely and appropriate action."

As I NOW CONSIDER THAT eight-week period from the end of the Tailhook Symposium in early September to the days immediately following my visit to the Navy IG, it seems almost unbelievable how quickly events had happened which would, in large measure, set the tone and determine the course of action over the next several years. Arguably, the beginning event was an early-morning breakfast meeting on Tailhook departure day, Sunday, September 8, 1991, in the Las Vegas Hilton Hotel. It had been attended by my Naval Academy classmate, Rear Adm. Jack Snyder, USN, his aide, Lt. Paula Coughlin, USN, and several other members of his staff.

Adm. Snyder's position was that of the commander, Naval Air Test Center, Naval Air Station Patuxent River, Maryland. He had only recently been promoted to his present rank and assumed command a few months later in July 1991. This was a choice assignment for a naval aviator and was seen as fitting for Snyder whose career to date had been exemplary. Snyder was a highly decorated fighter pilot who had commanded VF-1, an F-14 Tomcat Fighter

Squadron, the "Wolfpack," when it was awarded the Clifton Award as the Best Fighter Squadron in the Navy in 1983. That same year, he was named the Fighter Pilot of the Year. He later commanded VF-124, the "Gunfighters," the F-14 Master Training Squadron located at "Fightertown USA"—Naval Air Station Miramar, California. Significantly, he had also served as president of the Tailhook Association from 1985–1987.

That two-year stint had afforded him a unique perspective into the evolving culture and politics of the Tailhook symposiums and the naval aviator attendees. Indeed, in 1985, he had to personally address a crisis which had been brought to his attention by Vice Adm. Edward H. Martin, Deputy Chief of Naval Operations (Air Warfare). The Air Boss had sent a blistering letter of condemnation about the recent Tailhook to the commander, Naval Air Force, Pacific Fleet (COMNAVAIRPAC). He wanted his "message to Garcia" to be broadcast loud and clear throughout Naval Aviation. In part, he wrote,

> The general decorum and conduct last year were far less than that expected of mature naval officers. Certain observers even described some of the activity in the hotel halls and suites as grossly appalling, a "rambunctious drunken melee." There was virtually no responsibility displayed by anyone in an attempt to restrain those who were getting out of hand. Heavy drinking and other excesses were not only condoned, they were encouraged by some organizations. We can ill afford this type of behavior and indeed must not must tolerate it. The Navy, not the individual, his organization, or the Tailhook Organization, is charged with the events and certainly will be cast in disreputable light. Let's get the word out that each individual will be held accountable for his or her actions and also is responsible to exercise common sense and leadership to ensure that his squadron mates and associates conduct

> themselves in accordance with norms expected of naval officers. We will not condone institutionalized indiscretions.[1]

It was Capt. Snyder's responsibility to address and respond to Vice Adm. Martin's letter, and he did so by outlining, in a six-page letter, the steps he would take to institutionalize the necessary changes to get things back under control. One of them resulted in a letter sent by Snyder to all squadron COs prior to the Tailhook in 1986 admonishing them that unacceptable behavior would not be condoned.

Reports and stories published at the time emanating from various organizations and from a variety of "sources" quoted in respected publications offer different versions of what was said and not said at that breakfast staff meeting at the Hilton. The preponderance of evidence clearly supports a finding that it is highly likely that even if his female flag lieutenant, Lt. Coughlin, did first mention her Saturday-night encounter with aviators at the third-floor gauntlet, she expressed it in such a way as to not elicit anything more than a casual response from anyone at the breakfast table.

It was not until nearly two weeks later in his Patuxent River office that Adm. Snyder was fully briefed on the details of Lt. Coughlin's assault at Tailhook by his deputy, Capt. Robert Parkinson. This is a very important point because in the time period of this part of the Tailhook story, there was little difference in the narratives between what Snyder and Coughlin were saying about when and under what circumstances she had initially described her gauntlet attack to him.

However, as more officials and politicians were becoming informed and involved and the story was working its way up the chain of command and conversations were being made "on the record," Lt. Coughlin's account became significantly different. Ultimately, she portrayed Snyder as no less than insensitive, indifferent, or unconcerned about her welfare.

Her eventual account had her first telling Snyder about the attack during a telephone conversation before the Hilton breakfast. Shortly after that supposed telephone conversation, she purportedly repeated the same story while at the staff breakfast. In both instances, according to her, his response was curt and derisive, which left her bewildered and angry. Whenever and to whomever she told this modified version, there is little doubt that the listener would conclude that Snyder had become the villain.

On the other hand, Snyder continued to maintain throughout this period and afterward that he first heard from her what had happened to her on the Hilton's third floor was at the meeting with Coughlin on September 19—the day after he had been briefed by his executive officer.

That meeting took place in the admiral's office and was attended by Adm. Snyder, Lt. Coughlin, and Capt. Parkinson. Lt. Coughlin told the following story of what happened to her on Saturday night: after the conclusion of the awards dinner and after leaving the Hilton event, she went back to her nearby hotel, the Paddle Wheel, and changed clothes into casual attire. She soon returned to the Hilton where she planned to meet fellow aviators at the hospitality suites on the third floor. Upon entering the corridor near the elevators from the patio area around 11:30 PM, she soon encountered the gauntlet and graphically described to Snyder and Parkinson the sexual assault committed by her perpetrators.

There was a full and frank discussion between the admiral and his aide during the meeting. In the end, it was mutually agreed that Adm. Snyder would contact and fully inform several senior officials as to what had taken place at Tailhook regarding Lt. Coughlin: Capt. Frederick Ludwig, a fellow fighter pilot who was the president of the Tailhook Association, Vice Adm. Dunleavy, the head of Naval Aviation, and Vice Adm. William Bowes, the head of the Naval Air Systems Command, who was Snyder's next-in-line superior officer. Additionally, both he and his flag lieutenant would write separate letters to Adm. Dunleavy requesting a formal investigation.

Ten days later, on September 29, 1991, Adm. Snyder went to the Pentagon and hand carried both letters to Adm. Dunleavy who, after reading them, delivered the letters to his superior in his chain of command, Adm. Jerome Johnson, vice chief of Naval Operations. But unbeknownst to either Snyder or Dunleavy, days earlier, Lt.

Coughlin had already shared her descriptive letter with a friend who worked at BUPERS (the Bureau of Naval Personnel). Her letter soon made its way to the head of that organization, Vice Adm. Jeremy Boorda. The results of his personal involvement would be immediate and dramatic. Lt. Coughlin would soon be removed from her position on the staff of Adm. Snyder and be temporarily assigned to duties at BUPERS. Meanwhile, Adm. Boorda became a powerful and dedicated opponent of Adm. Snyder. There is little doubt that as the Navy's top "people person," Adm. Boorda's recommendations carried significant importance in the personnel assignment decisions of Adm. Frank Kelso, the Navy's Chief of Naval Operations.

As a result, on November 4, 1991, a Navy press release announced that the CNO was temporarily relieving Adm. Snyder of his command as head of the Naval Air Test Center. Six weeks later, on December 20, 1991, Adm. Kelso announced the relief permanent citing Adm. Snyder's "lack of timely action in directing an investigation into certain events at the 1991 Tailhook Association in Las Vegas," according to the Navy spokesperson, Lt. Fred Hanley. Adm. Snyder was temporarily assigned to the Naval Air Systems Command.

There is a catchphrase naval expression, banal though it is, that is often used in circumstances like this and was, in fact, uttered by many officials and commentators: "the Chief had lost confidence in the ability of one his officers [Rear Adm. Snyder] to successfully lead his organization." On the other hand, there were many in the armed services who shared the opinion that what had happened to Adm. Snyder was both unjust and unfair. He had become a political victim when the Navy had needed a scapegoat. Of course, many were hoping that his fall would be the one and only. They could hardly have imagined that his was just the tip of the iceberg of what would become a very long list of men whose distinguished careers would be abruptly and unceremoniously ended.

This, unfortunately, was not the only Tailhook-related story which was unfolding. Soon after reading Lt. Coughlin's letter on September 29, 1991, the VCNO, Adm. Johnson, also a naval aviator, summoned Rear Adm. Duvall M. Williams, the head of the

Naval Investigative Service (NIS), an organization composed of some 1,100 civilian inspectors. His office, like that of the Navy IG, is located in the Washington Navy Yard. The eventual outcome of that meeting was that a criminal investigation was begun on October 11, 1991, which focused solely on identifying and then prosecuting Lt. Coughlin's attackers as well as other participants in the gauntlet.*

It was the ultimate in irony that on this same October day, Capt. Ludwig (call sign, "Wigs"), president of the Tailhook Association, dispatched his Tailhook "debrief" letter in which he described the "good" and the "others" to the commanding officers of all naval aviation squadrons.[2] While just the opening paragraph details all the good things which took place over the course of the three-day event, the remaining five paragraphs detailed examples of irresponsible and unprofessional behavior. He raised the issue of the gauntlet and told the squadron COs that he had received "distressing" reports about its female victims.

Curiously, while Ludwig urged his readers to get the word out to all naval aviators that unacceptable behavior would not be condoned or tolerated by the organization, he suggested no other corrective actions—other than he would "do damage control work at regaining our rapport with the Las Vegas Hilton."

In hindsight, it is clear that months before, Capt. Ludwig correctly anticipated the "others" and must have thought he had established adequate safeguards to prevent their occurrence. In his pre-Tailhook, August 15, 1991 letter to the squadron "Tailhook representatives," he cautioned about the problems associated with "late-night gang mentality" and encouraged the reps to be proactive.[3] He advised them that, if necessary, they should contact hotel security or nearby Association officials for help in solving any problems. In his penultimate paragraph, he raises the issue of personal conduct emphasizing that "*lewd and lascivious*" behavior is unacceptable. In retrospect, it was obvious that there were many Tailhook attendees who either never "got the word" or failed to heed it.

---

* The function of the Naval Investigative Service (NIS) was to gather information necessary for the pursuit of criminal cases for Navy prosecutors. In 1992, the NIS became the Naval Criminal Investigative Service (NCIS).

While Capt. Ludwig's August 15 letter may not have produced the desired results, his October 11 debrief letter was producing results he could not have foreseen. On October 28, 1991, the Secretary of the Navy, H. Lawrence Garrett III, received a copy of Ludwig's letter, and after discussions with Adm. Kelso, the CNO, sent Ludwig a letter the following day.[4] In it, he expressed his outrage and anger over the " personal abuses, behavioral excesses, and quite possibly criminal conduct that took place at Tailhook '91 and have now been reported to me." In what can only be described as delivering a bombshell, Garrett, himself a naval aviator who had attended Tailhook '91, immediately severed all Navy support for the Tailhook Association.

While that letter effectively ended an era, another of his letters on the same day began something which would have major consequences—the very least of which was my recent visit to the Navy IG. For it was on that day that Sec. Garrett sent a memorandum to the Undersecretary of the Navy, Dan Howard, instructing him to task the Navy IG "to conduct a thorough investigation of any noncriminal abuses or violations of law or regulations that might be associated with the Tailhook Association, or subject Symposium."[5] Later that day, the undersecretary responded to the Garrett directive by promulgating his own memorandum to the Navy IG, directing him to conduct an investigation into the "organization and support of the Tailhook Organization" including a wide array of related issues.[6] Of significance was his explicit instruction that "any evidence of criminal misconduct should be referred to the commander, Naval Investigative Service, for appropriate action." He directed the IG to complete the investigation in thirty days.

The Navy secretary and his staff weren't the only high-level officials who had recently read Capt. Ludwig's explosive October 11 letter. His letter and Lt. Coughlin's letter were being read by an ever-expanding group of influential people throughout Washington, DC. On October 29, 1991, the very same day as the SECNAV's letter and memo and the UnderSECNAV's memo, Lt. Coughlin visited Sen. John McCain at his Senate office to "discuss a matter of great urgency to her." A two-hour conversation ensued.

Immediately following her office visit, Sen. McCain went directly to the floor of the Senate, where he delivered a blistering condemnation of those who were involved in the actions described in Capt. Ludwig's letter and Lt. Coughlin's meeting.[7] Having asked that Ludwig's entire letter become a part of the Senate record, he quoted from several of its passages, which described the damages incurred, the gauntlet, and the physical abuses and molestations. He said that he had contacted Navy Sec. Garrett as well as Secretary of Defense Cheney and urged them to fully investigate all the incidents. He was "appalled and offended by the aviators' actions against the women involved." Continuing, he asked, "Why hadn't anything been done yet by the Navy?" and urged its leaders to terminate all ties with the Tailhook Organization until the authorities had completed a "prompt and thorough investigation…and those responsible for these incidents be given appropriate punishment."

The circumstances surrounding how and why this highly unusual but significantly important meeting took place are much in dispute. Lt. Coughlin has never gone on record and declined a request to explain her version of how it came about. On the other hand, Sen. McCain, in an October 1996 PBS *Frontline* interview entitled "The Navy Blues," said that "a Navy senate liaison officer had arranged the meeting," but there is no evidence which supports that claim.[8] It might be just a remarkable coincidence that Sen. McCain's last job as a Navy captain prior to his retirement in 1981 was, in fact, senate liaison in the Navy's Office of Legislative Affairs.

What is not in dispute, however, is that a close political relationship between Lt. Coughlin and her Senate defender, McCain, developed shortly after their initial meeting and lasted throughout his 1992 Senate reelection campaign. Political commentators agreed that the feminine vote was an important element in his reelection. Now having such a famous feminist issue strong public statements supporting him was a very effective counter to his opponent's charges that he was, after all, just "one of the boys" whose reputation was as both a "hell-raiser" and "womanizer."

Watching Sen. McCain deliver his passionate address on a C-SPAN rebroadcast, I was instantly reminded of my association with him. The senator graduated from the Naval Academy in 1958 and I in 1966. The first time I met him was when he was an instructor in the pilot training command at NAS Meridian, Mississippi, in 1967, and I was a student naval aviator (SNA). His reputation as a "screamer" was well deserved as he showed little tolerance for the mistakes his students had made. Our paths crossed many times since then.

One such event occurred in 1989 when I was an Eastern Airline pilot representative of the Airline Pilot Association (ALPA), I had been "volunteered" to lobby Sen. McCain because of our past mutual associations. At the time, the three unions representing Eastern employees were on strike against Mr. Francisco Lorenzo, whom many considered to be the airline industry's living version of *Wall Street's* Gordon Gecko—Mr. Greed personified. At the time, the Senate was considering a bill establishing a "Presidential Emergency Board," which would have ended the crippling strike and authorized the Board to settle the dispute. The unions had supported the move, but Lorenzo was adamantly opposed to it.

There was a full court press by ALPA to garner the support of several swing Republican votes as *sixty* was the crucial number to effectively pass the legislation by overriding the expected veto of President George H. W. Bush. I was but one of many Eastern Airline pilots dispatched by ALPA one day to visit various senators in their Washington offices. I had gone alone to Sen. McCain's Senate office to meet with him. I sat in his lobby for hours until he finally relented and agreed to see me. I had brought with me personal and group letters and signed petitions from several of his fellow Hanoi Hilton POWs who were Eastern pilots, naval aviator buddies, and USNA classmates. Many of them were close friends of his and mine, all asking him to "do the right thing." I was convinced in my own mind that if anything were to change his mind from making a purely political decision, it would be the testimonials which I had given him. I had hoped that he would join all his Democratic and several Republican colleagues in supporting the bill.

After he had read most of the material, I remember him saying, "I have never been more impressed with these messages from friends whom I know and admire, but I can't support your position." When I asked him why, he admitted that Lorenzo and Frank Borman, his Eastern predecessor, had played important roles in financially backing his campaigns, and therefore, he owed his benefactors his allegiance. He was not going to change his mind. Upon hearing that, I stood up, held up my left hand, pointed to the Naval Academy ring on my finger, and asked him, "Doesn't this mean anything, senator?" When he made no reply, I turned and left his office bitterly disappointed and saddened by what I believed to be his unethical and ignoble decision.

To recap, by early November, the NIS and IG organizations were conducting investigations whose initial deadlines were December 15, 1991, and November 29, 1991, respectively. The long-standing and close relationship between the Navy and the Tailhook Association was severed. The civilian and military leadership at both the Navy and Defense Departments were now fully engaged in responding to the media and Congress. Rear Adm. Snyder had become the first casualty of the scandal. Without question, many of the aviators who had attended the Tailhook symposium were now shaking their heads asking, "How the hell could this have happened?"—just like me!

The next afternoon, I was one of two first officers, along with our captain, who were scheduled to fly a Boeing 767/300 from Dulles to Rome on an all-nighter. After a twenty-four-hour layover, we would them then fly a short flight to Milan where we would stay for another twenty-four hours before returning to Dulles.

Since this would be my first time back in Rome in over twenty years, I was really looking forward to retracing steps which I had taken as a Navy lieutenant in 1970 during the USS *Saratoga*'s port visit to nearby Naples. The highpoint of my four-day visit to Rome and Vatican City was when I was privileged to have a private audience with Pope Paul VI in St. Peter's Basilica (my mom prominently displayed the picture of the pope and me on her bedroom wall right below her cherished crucifix).

This was one of several memorable events from that cruise during which *Sara* visited many of the great Mediterranean seaport cities, including Barcelona, Palma de Mallorca, Ville de France,

Malta, Athens, Corfu, and Rhodes. I also got to visit Tripoli, Libya, where I was temporarily stationed at Wheelus Air Force Base. I flew simulated bombing missions to desert targets twice a day for four days. As a result of Col. Muammar Gadafi overthrowing the king and assuming control, the US base was eventually turned over to him a few months later.

Flying low level over the Med's islands and coastlines in an A-7 was quite a treat. We often had joint air operations with planes from England, France and other NATO allies. And of course, we always had Russian ships sailing nearby and witnessed occasional Russian "Bear" aircraft overflights. One afternoon while operating off the French coast, my squadron operations officer informed me that I had been assigned escort duty the next day as several VIPs were coming aboard *Sara*.

As I had LSO duty the next day, I was on the platform when the ship's transport plane (the COD) successfully trapped aboard mid-morning. Shortly after we finished "trapping" the rest of the planes, I was summoned to the captain's office where I was introduced to my VIP: eight-year-old Prince Albert, son of Prince Rainier and Princess Grace of Monaco. My duty was to show him around the ship for four hours while his father was being hosted by the admiral and commanding officer.

I tried my best to show him as much of the ship as I could, including all those places I normally "hang out." I took him to the "Stinger Ready Room," the Carrier Air Traffic Control Center (CATCC), Pri-Fly (the home of the Air Boss), Vultures' Row (the observation deck high above the flight deck where one can watch the landings), the "dirty shirt" wardroom where aviators eat their meals, the flight deck and the "LSO platform" as I still had LSO duty that afternoon. The time, literally, flew by, and at 3:00 PM, I returned the prince to the Air Ops office where he was reunited with his father's entourage. As we said our good-byes, he thanked me and said he had a wonderful time. He asked if he could come back and do it again. I assured him he could, "Just ask your father to arrange it."

My layover time in Rome and Milan was primarily spent on walking tours. The cities' sights and sounds were fantastic. And the food and drinks were even better than I had remembered them to be. As I was relaxing in my copilot seat looking down on the western coast of Ireland as we flew home, I thought how lucky and fortunate I was to be able to have all these incredible experiences.

The Dark Ages

"Those responsible will be held accountable."

During my years at the "Boat School" in the sixties, the three-month period of time from after Christmas leave (i.e., vacation) to the beginning of Easter leave was appropriately named: the "Dark Ages." It was mostly because of the cold, damp, and otherwise gloomy weather, which permeated into every facet of a midshipman's life. In the same period in 1992, for Naval Aviation and naval aviators, it was far more than just the weather.

The mostly civilian NIS and IG investigators were deployed to Naval and Marine Corps air stations throughout the United States and to foreign lands to conduct their investigations and interviews. Many had even gone aboard aircraft carriers stationed overseas. Their reports were ultimately provided to their uniformed bosses back in DC who were meeting in the Pentagon.

Navy Sec. Garrett had delegated Undersecretary Howard the authority to oversee the conduct of both investigations. In the beginning, the undersecretary had received separate weekly briefings from the leaders of the NIS and IG, but eventually, those briefings were combined into a single weekly meeting. In attendance were Mr. Dan Howard, the undersecretary; Rear Adm. "Mac" Williams, NIS; Rear Adm. George Davis, IG; Rear Adm. Ted Gordon, Navy JAG; and,

Ms. Barbara Pope, asst. sec. for Manpower and Reserve Affairs. Senior members of their staffs were also included on an "as needed" basis.

Since assuming command of the Reserve IG unit in October, I had been spending one weekend per month plus, on average, two additional nonweekend days at the IG offices. I was very fortunate to have gifted and conscientious Reserve officers and petty officers whom I relied upon to help me get up to speed as quickly as possible in my new assignment. Realizing I had more than a passing interest in the IG's Tailhook investigation, I made it known to all the reservists in my command that I thought it best not to brief me about anything they heard, saw, or read relating to Tailhook as part of their official duties unless they thought I had a need to know. If that were the case, I advised them to first bring their issue to my executive officer, Capt. Denny McHugh. In civilian life, Denny was a Maryland district court judge, so I had complete confidence in his ability to handle what might be a difficult decision. Fortunately, during my two-year tenure as CO, not once did I ever have a conversation about Tailhook with anyone at the IG office save for the ones I had with Rear Adm. Davis and his two investigators back in October.

Of course, my self-imposed restrictions with respect to the IG office did not preclude me from reading about Tailhook in the Washington newspapers and other publications. Neither was I prevented from engaging in conversations with other naval aviators or listening to or reading the "scuttlebutt" about what was going on in the "fleet," and increasingly, there was a lot to consume. There were developing two fundamentally separate and distinct story lines even though, at the core, both had to do with the Navy. One concerned what was going on inside the Capital Beltway—specifically within the Pentagon offices of the Navy leadership. The other was what was taking place in the most fundamental structure of Naval Aviation, the squadron, and was happening literally around the world.

While the number of players engaged in the inside story wasn't very large, their weekly interaction was a source of much talk and speculation. Every week, Admirals Williams of the NIS and Davis of the IG were the providers and distributors of the information which their organizations were gathering. Sec. Howard was the principal overseer while Sec. Pope was, in effect, an additional overseer but one whose power was far less than Howard's. Finally, Adm. Gordon, as the Navy JAG, was there to ensure that the discussions and decisions took place in accordance with Navy procedures and directives and the UCMJ. On paper, it appeared to be an efficient and well-planned group which would ultimately provide a factual, insightful, and comprehensive report of Tailhook. Unfortunately, that proved to not be the case.

Some of the initial scuttlebutt was that there were serious and very personal conflicts among members of the review group. The most talked about was that which seemed to exist between Sec. Pope and Rear Adm. Williams. Their apparent enmity centered on vastly different opinions of women in the military. Rear Adm. Williams's strongly held view that women had, at best, only a minor role in Naval Aviation was in sharp contrast with Sec. Pope's position that there should be no barriers to women in any role in the Navy. On several occasions, angry and heated exchanges between the two were rumored to have continued into the Pentagon corridors after the meetings had adjourned.

After both the NIS and NIG reports' original deadlines had passed, additional rumors began to surface, which clearly suggested there were serious problems with the inquiry itself. Both organizations' investigators had come to a number of conclusions, which they had brought to their superiors' attention but were subsequently never sufficiently addressed nor solved by the group.

On one hand, the scope of the IG inquiry was essentially two-fold: to investigate the *noncriminal* (1) relationship between the Navy and the Tailhook Organization and (2) the conduct of the symposium. Further, their directive was "*any evidence of criminal misconduct should be referred to the NIS for appropriate action.*"[9] The limited number of IG investigators concluded early on that their role should be expanded to include pursuing individual UCMJ prohibited acts or behavior. To do so, they realized, would have required additional manpower, which their organization didn't possess. Further, there was a serious coordination problem. Because of established procedural hurdles which were never solved, the IG investigators weren't able to pass on to their NIS counterparts the information which they had uncovered related to criminal misconduct.

On the other hand, the NIS investigators were quickly discovering that identifying those who assaulted Lt. Coughlin as well as those who participated in the gauntlet were far more difficult tasks than they originally thought. The investigation had been assigned to the assistant special agent in charge of the NIS office at her duty station, NAS Patuxent River, but agents worldwide were necessarily involved. No aviators were coming forward and volunteering any information which might aid them. Just like the IG inspectors, the NIS agents were uncovering many examples of noncriminal behavior but otherwise prohibited by the UCMJ, which they couldn't pursue because of the limited scope of their marching orders.

The other story was taking place in Navy and Marine Corps squadron ready rooms around the world. Armed with a list of nearly two thousand symposium attendees provided by the Tailhook Association, the NIS inspectors would arrive at an air base such as NAS Miramar or NAS Lemoore and begin their interview process. Of course, their arrival was widely anticipated, and the news of them reporting aboard quickly spread throughout all the squadrons based there. In anticipation of what would take place, every squadron had conducted an "all-hands" meeting, which addressed the rights, responsibilities, etc., of the interviewees. Normally, the squadron's CO, XO, and legal officer would take part. Members of the Navy JAG community assigned to the base might also be included in these discussions to provide "expert advice."

As a former squadron CO, I realized what difficult moral, ethical, and legal questions surrounded this undertaking. On one hand, I thought that if officers had firsthand knowledge of information about criminal assaults and other crimes especially committed against fellow officers, they had an obligation to provide it to the investigators. On the other hand, I knew that the incredibly strong bonds of loyalty and trust between squadron mates and comrades might very well prevent the disclosure of incriminating information. This was especially the case because of a subgroup organization within each squadron normally referred to as JOPA, which stood for Junior Officer Protection Association.

For those of us who were "ring knockers" (aka, Naval Academy grads), the lone precept of JOPA was essentially the same tenet we learned during our Plebe summer and was aptly summed up: "Whatever you do, you don't bilge your classmate." Said another way, "You don't squeal on your buddy."

Additionally, there were also the potential conflicting issues of the exertion of "command influence" by squadron CO's and other superior officers and the need to respect every officer's rights afforded under the UCMJ. Clearly, these dilemmas were being necessarily addressed and thought through very carefully by every naval officer before he or she was interviewed. I had but one instance in my thirty-year career when I dealt with NIS investigators, and unfortunately, that episode did not leave me with a good feeling of how this all might turn out. At best I thought it would provide mixed results.

Increasingly, during this period, in McGarvey's or around the academy or on my airline flights, I'd engage an active duty JO naval aviator who'd relate to me his firsthand story or one which he heard about the NIS interview process. Generally, the interview would start out very friendly and the questions would be simple and straightforward: asking about what events, times, dates did you attend; what did you witness; whom do you remember seeing; whom were you with, etc. Since the investigators initially had little incriminating evidence to rely on, they desperately needed the help of aviators to track down the perpetrators. Although many acknowledged their presence on the patio, in certain of the suites and the third-floor corridor, hardly anyone admitted to seeing or being part of the gauntlet group which they were hoping to identify. Moreover, the harder they pushed for this type information, the more resistance they received from their interviewee. As a result, the word swiftly spread throughout the aviation community that the investigators were conducting a "witch hunt" in which everyone was a suspect and no junior officer would be spared.

Even though the Dark Ages had officially ended in "Crabtown by the Bay" days earlier, and the weather had begun to improve significantly, the gloom was continuing for the Naval Aviation community. Before he left on a two-week official trip to Australia where he would represent the US in the commemoration of the fiftieth anniversary of the famous and significant World War II Battle of the Coral Sea, Sec. Garrett received final briefings on the IG and NIS reports, now months overdue from the heads of the two organizations. Although both reports were now just about ready for distribution on April 28, his direction was to not release them to the public until they were entirely complete. Unfortunately, after he departed, leaks of the reports were taking place and showing up in various influential newspapers. Fearful that this would do more unnecessary damage to the Navy, UnderSec. Howard released them on April 30.

The initial reaction by the Congress, press, and other interested parties was almost universally negative. The two reports provided more than enough fodder for critics of all types, persuasions and motivations. On one hand, the IG report detailed all sorts of inappropriate and objectionable behavior by the younger naval aviators. It also addressed the unlawful use of government planes to carry convention attendees to and from Las Vegas from naval air stations all over the US. The pervasive abuse of alcohol and the widespread perception of female aviators as second-class citizens were topics which received strong condemnation in the report.

On the other hand, the NIS report, containing more than two thousand pages, was the product of more than 2,100 officer interviews hardly any of which were of or about "senior" officers—the many squadron commanders, captains, and admirals who were there. The overwhelming majority were lieutenants and lieutenants (junior grade) who were questioned. Most significantly, the report identified less than five individuals whom they wanted to pursue as possible perpetrators of the alleged attacks against Lt. Coughlin.

Inadequate, *irresponsible*, and *halfhearted* were some of the nicer terms which some officials were using to describe the reports. Unfortunately, *whitewash*, *sham*, and *unbelievable* were words used far more frequently by congressmen, especially, to describe the results of the six-month-long investigations. In sum, no one was pleased or satisfied with the results—including the secretary of the Navy, who from the moment he returned from his trip, was keenly aware that something more had to be done and the sooner the better.

Reacting to pressure from inside the Navy, the Pentagon, the Congress, the White House, and the press, SECNAV Garrett spent many hours with his advisors in May seeking to address the reports' shortcomings and inadequacies. There was an important additional member, SECNAV's own attorney, Mr. Craig King, the Navy general counsel to the frequent meetings attended by the heads of the NIS, IG, and JAG. Although the NIS and IG had already referred individual prosecutable cases identified in their reports for disciplinary or administrative action to the commanders of the Atlantic and Pacific fleets, the group proposed additional steps to be taken and ways to accomplish them. Unfortunately, it wasn't until late in May that a plan was accepted and approved by Sec. Garrett, and it was based on the recommendations contained in the JAG's Memorandum of May 22, 1992.[10]

Previously, on May 14, SECNAV had directed Rear Adm. Gordon to review the NIS and IG reports and provide "options that would permit individuals to be held accountable for actions within those investigations." Then on June 2, 1992, SECNAV sent a memorandum to the chief of Naval Operations and the commandant of the Marine Corps whose subject was "*behavior and attitudes toward women.*"[11]

Clearly, the secretary was angry with the criminal behavior of certain of the aviators while at Tailhook and even more so afterward during the interview process by their lack of truthfulness and accountability. He also widened the ongoing investigations to include all twenty-six squadron commanding officers who were responsible for their third-floor hospitality suites. Along with CINCLANTFLT and CINCPACFLT, he additionally tasked the chief of Naval Education and Training and the director of the Naval Reserve, with the assistance of the Navy's general counsel, to ensure that all these COs would be interviewed and appropriate action be taken. SECNAV ended the memo expressing confidence that like the similar social problems of racial discrimination and drug abuse, "the battle for opportunities and respect for women...will be successful."

(The JAG's Memo of May 22, 1992 detailing his analysis and providing options to those in the chain of command was included as an attachment to the memorandum).

While the Navy had decided its own response in the Pentagon, a few miles away on Capitol Hill also on June 2, members of the Senate Armed Services Committee (SASC), normally strong Navy backers, were about to exercise their authority over the Navy. Clearly outraged by what they had heard and read about Tailhook and frustrated by the Navy's apparent inability to solve its problems as outlined in the IG and NIS reports, some senators had decided it was time to get more involved.

At a Senate Armed Services Subcommittee on Manpower and Personnel Hearing, which was addressing "Military Manpower Issues in the FY '93 DoD Authorization," Chairman John Glenn and Ranking Minority Member John McCain took dead aim at Asst. Sec. Pope and asked tough accusatory questions about the Navy's handling of and response to several recent well-publicized events: the sexual assaults at the Orlando Training Center, the Naval Academy, and especially Tailhook. Regarding Tailhook, "Can you assure us that someone in authority will be held accountable?"[12] was the question asked by Sen. Glenn that was at the core of their concern. Ms. Pope replied with certitude to the senators that "those responsible will be held accountable." Despite the obfuscation, lies, and closing of ranks as outlined in the IG report, she and the Navy secretary were confident that steps now being implemented by the investigators would result in many officers being appropriately disciplined.

Quite unexpectedly, the powerful SASC Chairman, Sen. Sam Nunn, took a seat at the table and when recognized, engaged Ms. Pope about the Tailhook accountability issue and related it directly to the SASC's authority over officer promotions. He told her that all promotion lists currently before the committee for approval would not be acted upon until the committee received assurance that every officer on the lists was not involved in any way with the wrongdoings at Tailhook or the ongoing investigations. This message was as clear as it was stunning—the SASC will force the Navy into dealing immediately with the guilt or innocence of those officers associated in any way with Tailhook or its aftermath.

On that same day, the SASC issued two letters, signed by Chairman Nunn and Ranking Minority Member John Warner, himself a former Navy secretary, to Defense Sec. Cheney, which would have severe and long-lasting consequences.[13] The first directed the DoD to interview all the COs of the squadrons which had third-floor hospitality suites. More significantly and certainly more alarmingly, the second letter informed the secretary that the committee had "frozen" all Navy and Marine Corps promotions—the immediate effect was to hold up more than 4,500. In order to be promoted, the DoD was required to certify that the particular officer either was not in any way associated with Tailhook, or if he or she were, their complete file was to be furnished to the committee (when this happened the officer's record would henceforth be "flagged").

This produced a shock wave throughout the entire Navy because this wasn't a freeze on just naval and marine aviators—it was on *all* Navy and Marine Corps officers. When I first heard about this action, I was incredulous that the Senate would take such a dramatic and drastic step. In my thirty years in the Navy, I had never witnessed nor heard about such a sweeping decree that would affect every officer—some immediately but most eventually. I had thought of myself as being in the latter category but really didn't give it much thought.

However, a few months later, while attending a formal Navy "dining out" event in Washington, DC, I witnessed firsthand the unintended consequences of the freeze. Part of the elaborate affair, attended by officers and their wives, husbands, or guests, is the final toasting. I was preselected to offer the toast to the chief of Naval Operations which I did when it was my turn. Two "toasters" after me was a Naval Academy classmate (not an aviator) who chose to toast Naval Aviation and "those intrepid airmen who honored us at Tailhook which brought us our new promotion procedures." He must have thought that his performance was either humorous or clever by the look on his face. I was furious, and had we been alone, I'm certain I would have had, at the very least, some choice words for him. As it was, there followed a very pregnant pause before everyone seemed to recoup and the remaining toasts were offered. As I was leaving the banquet a short time later, I thought about confronting my classmate and reading him the riot act but decided against it. In a way, I realized that all of us had already been affected by the "freeze."

The Boss and SECNAV Step Down

"When Irish eyes are smiling."

THE CHILLING EFFECTS ON NAVY morale brought on by the double-barrel blasts of the two recent events—broadening and intensifying the investigations and holding up the promotions—were widespread and significant throughout the entire Navy organization. While the ranking Navy and Marine Corps officers continued to put on their best faces and tried to assure everyone that "all was well," it seemed to many that the entire enterprise was at "general quarters." And then to make matters worse, from inside the beltway, stories began to circulate that only exacerbated the level of angst and concern.

From the very beginning of the Tailhook saga, it was a well-known fact that both Sec. Garrett and CNO Kelso had attended the symposium. Many of us had actually seen them socializing at the informal get-togethers. During the initial NIS investigation, there were statements made to and recorded by agents that placed SECNAV at or near the area where the gauntlet took place. However, neither of the reports released in April contained details of their activities or whereabouts. Having received press inquiries requesting these details, SECNAV's office, on June 8, released a statement that denied knowledge of or witnessing any inappropriate behavior. These inquiries also sparked an internal search conducted by the vice chief, Adm. Jerry Johnson.

In short order, he was subsequently briefed by his staff about part of a previously unpublished fifty-five-page "supplemental" NIS investigation report, which was completed after the April 30 release. One file, contained therein, included the testimony of a marine officer who stated that he witnessed the secretary in the now infamous Rhino suite on Saturday evening after the formal concluding dinner.

The Marine Corps Tactical Reconnaissance Squadron 3 (VMFP-3), whose mascot was a rhinoceros, sponsored a third-floor suite at the Hilton. Its centerpiece was an eight-foot mural of a rhino that sported a dildo which dispensed an alcoholic drink called Rhino Spunk.

After Sec. Garrett was informed of this potentially damaging revelation which put him "at the scene of some of the crimes," he asked the Department of Defense Inspector General (DoD IG) on June 10 to investigate why this file had been missing from the initial report. (He could easily have directed his own NIS to do this, but this would have raised serious questions regarding the apparent conflict of interest where the same organization would be investigating itself[14]).

The next day on June 11, he issued a two-page sworn statement which first described the reason why he was making it and then provided all the details he recalled concerning his activities on the evening of Saturday, September 7, 1991.[15]

According to this document, after delivering his banquet speech, he retired to his Hilton Hotel room where he changed into casual clothes. He then proceeded to the third-floor patio area where he joined "hundreds of Tailhook attendees" and remained there for about forty-five minutes. Although he flatly denied visiting or spending time in "any of the various suites on the third floor," he acknowledged that he "took a can of beer...from a container of beverages" located at the poolside entrance to one of the suites. He did not recall talking to anyone "while I was in the area of the entrance to this suite, although I may have." He concluded the statement saying that he did not observe any inappropriate or offensive conduct.

Upon reading his statement, while I thought he obviously made it to clarify his situation, in reality, I thought it significantly intensified the focus of many leaders, the Congress, and the press on the "missing" supplemental report itself.

For weeks, I had known about and planned to attend the change of command and retirement of my old boss, Vice Adm. Dunleavy. It was to take place on June 12 at the Washington Navy Yard—coincidentally where I was currently performing my Naval Reserve duties at the offices of the Navy IG. I had successfully rearranged my monthly flight schedule to get the day off by trading my trips to Paris with trips to London and Amsterdam with two copilots friends. I had also been chatting on the phone with my close friend, Adm. Jack Moriarty, who told me that he, too, was making plans to be in DC for the ceremony.

During several breakfast meetings with my 9:12 Annapolis buds, I had asked if any wanted to go with me to the ceremony. My friend Luke, ex-Air Force and current TWA captain, was the only taker. As a fellow New Englander from Marblehead, MA, Luke had met and socialized with Jack and Dick Dunleavy a number of times. He was part of the large group who were personal guests of Jack's when we were all aboard his command, the USS *John F. Kennedy*, during the relighting ceremony of the Statue of Liberty in New York harbor in 1986. A few weeks later, I travelled to Boston, where Luke was residing, and stayed with him for a few days.

Jack, with Adm. Dunleavy aboard, had sailed the *Kennedy* into Boston Harbor for a gala Beantown celebration.

For three wonderfully exciting days, Luke and I attended many of the official events aboard the ship and accompanied Jack and the Boss and several other friends and staff during several nights of socializing in some of Boston's most famous drinking and eating establishments. It was quite a memorable weekend!

The day had finally arrived, and Luke and I made the trip from Annapolis to DC in good time. After parking my car, we walked over to the nearby parade ground area where lots of uniformed officers were already seating themselves. We soon met and exchanged greetings with Adm. Jack and staked out some good seats. As I was surveying the crowd, it appeared that those in attendance were among the "who's who" of Naval Aviation. I recognized many former A-7 comrades of mine who were now wearing admiral stars and serving in leadership positions. I also saw two members of the Dunleavy family: the admiral's wife, Sibyl, and son, Mark. I was really looking forward to talking with both sometime after the ceremony.

The assistant chief of Naval Operations (Air) change of command soon commenced under glorious skies. It had all the pomp and circumstances of a regal performance. The highlight was, for many of us, the admiral's farewell speech. It was vintage Dunleavy—in a word, charming. His talk, however, was noticeably interrupted when the CNO, Adm. Kelso, arose from his front-row seat and suddenly departed the area. Dunleavy, seeing this, commented that "even the Boss sometimes gets called away." Without missing a beat, he immediately resumed his speech. At that instant, however, I wondered whether I was the only one saying to myself: "How incredibly awkward was that. I hope it was worth it."

It was a heartfelt and moving speech which ended with the Boss's usual exhortation: "Keep strokin'." I was left feeling both very proud and awfully sad. The concluding event was when the Navy Band, in all its splendor, marched away from the ceremonial area playing "When Irish Eyes Are Smiling"—a favorite of the Boss's. Although I couldn't notice, I'll bet I was not the only one who had to reach into a pocket to retrieve a handkerchief.

For a while after the ceremony ended, we three stood talking to one another about the speech. Occasionally, we were joined by friends of Jack or mine who had noticed us. At one point, I saw Sybil and Mark nearby and walked over to talk to them. While I received a very warm welcome from both, I told them how much I admired the Boss and how thankful I was to have known and worked for him. It was especially great to see Mark again. It had been four years since he graduated from the Academy, and we discussed his young career as an F/A-18 Hornet pilot.

He told me he was having a fantastic time enjoying every minute associated with carrier aviation. Kiddingly, I asked him if he recalled our conversation after I took him biplane flying inverted over sailboats in the Chesapeake Bay. He remembered it clearly as it was, he said, the first time he thought seriously about flying single-seat navy jets.

I had met Mark when he was in his third year at the US Naval Academy in the mid-eighties. His dream had been to go to flight school in Pensacola after graduation and win his Wings of Gold. At the time, his plan was to pilot the A-6 Intruder—the two-man aircraft in which his dad had been a B/N. In his senior year at the Boat School, I took Mark up in my Great Lakes open cockpit biplane a couple of times. It was hangared at the airport in Easton, Maryland, across the Chesapeake Bay from Annapolis. The flights took place on days when the weather was perfect: clear, sunny, and warm. We'd do lots of acrobatics and fly very low over the waters of the Chesapeake. Sailboats were plentiful, and these were great targets of opportunity for close flybys. Sailors frequently waived at us or in some cases saluted as we flew by the vessels. Occasionally, we were "flashed" by female crew members who were sunning in their bikinis.

After landing back at the Easton Airport, we jumped into my convertible corvette and drove back home to Annapolis. The forty-five-minute trip afforded us the opportunity to debrief our flight and do some serious "hangar flying." The point which I'd continue to make to him was that flying a single-seat fighter/attack airplane ought to be his goal. Trying to get him to rethink his current plan of flying the Intruder was not an easy sell, but my feeling was that he would at least consider the distinct advantages of piloting a single-seat aircraft. I reminded him that most single-seat jet jocks thought: "I'd rather have an extra two hundred pounds of gas instead of someone in back of or alongside me telling me what I should or shouldn't be doing."

After saying good-bye to Mark and Sybil, I rejoined Jack and Luke, and the three of us walked over to the nearby Navy Museum where the reception was taking place. After getting something to eat and drink, we mingled among the crowd. Occasionally, I'd run into an Academy classmate, shipmate, or squadron mate, and we'd chat for a few minutes about the "good old times" and, quite appropriately, Tailhook.

After a while, we saw that the Boss was in our vicinity and when he eventually saw us, came our way. For the next several minutes, we listened to him as he expressed his thanks to us—for our friendships as well as our support. In turn, we told him how appreciative we were to have known and worked for him and what a privilege it was for us to count him as a friend—and how much fun and all the good times we shared throughout the past years. Shortly after the Boss left us, Luke and I said our good-byes to Jack and headed back to Annapolis. In the words of the Boss: "What a great Navy Day!"

On the trip back home, Luke and I discussed the day's activities in general and several aspects in particular. The most interesting moment of the event for me was Adm. Kelso's sudden, unexplained, and most embarrassing exit. Whoever had summoned him and whatever the subject, it must have been so important that he couldn't have delayed his departure until the Boss completed his speech less than ten minutes later. I could only imagine that it must have been one of those very few individuals who were higher up in his extremely short chain of command.

On Tuesday, June 16, I flew my three-day trip to Amsterdam and had a great time visiting one of my favorite European cities. We landed at Schiphol Airport around 9:00 AM and got to our downtown hotel about an hour later. I spent most of the day sight-seeing on a rental bike—by far the most convenient and easiest way to see this fascinating city. Around 6:00 PM, the other copilot and I met in the hotel lobby bar and were soon joined by most of the flight attendants of our crew.

We then walked several blocks to a small and intimate restaurant, the *Black Swan*, owned and operated by two Danish friends of mine. Another of my Annapolis buddies, Pete Nevins, a former Navy and TWA pilot, had introduced me to them when they visited him in Annapolis in the late 1980s. Pete had retired early from TWA and opted to fly for KLM, based in Amsterdam, as a B747 copilot the last five years of his flying career. While living there, Pete had met and befriended Hans and his mate, Ellie. I had made it part of my routine to invite my crew to have dinner with me at their place whenever I was in their city on a layover.

The eight of us had a wonderful time being served and entertained by this joyful couple. The beer and wine, home-cooked food, and conversations were as good as anyone could remember. It was a single-choice menu which made ordering a no-brainer. Plus, because of its small size, we literally had the whole place to ourselves. Airline crews are renowned for locating and recording the best value eating places in every city around the world. Upon paying the modest check, all agreed that this place deserved to be added to that list.

We had an on-time arrival at Dulles, and I got back to my Annapolis condo early evening on the eighteenth. After unpacking, I settled in with a cocktail to get caught up on the latest Navy news from my favorite newspapers and messages left on my answering machine.

I soon learned that on the sixteenth, Sec. Garrett had further expanded his statement concerning his visit to the third-floor patio and hospitality suite area on Saturday night.[16] He reiterated that he neither saw nor heard any wrongdoing. On that same day, the NIS finally released their missing fifty-five-page supplemental report which included the file containing testimony which contradicted Garrett's recent statements.

The next day, Defense Sec. Cheney had issued a statement in support of his Navy secretary. While that vote of confidence must have been reassuring to Garrett, there were other stories suggesting that days before, on the twelfth, he had visited Cheney's office and had offered to resign over the revelation that there had been a missing report which contained incriminating information about him.

SECDEF had refused his offer, but the pressure must have been building considerably since the public release of the missing report. Learning about this meeting on the twelfth, I thought back to another event which I had witnessed on that same day—Adm. Kelso's, the CNO, awkward departure from the Boss's retirement ceremony at the Navy Yard. It might be just a coincidence, but it seemed reasonable to think that, all things considered, there was a distinct possibility that the two events were connected.

Factoring in all these new revelations only added to my feeling that this whole affair was, indeed, spinning out of control. I likened it to an aviation term that is all too often used by NTSB and other aircraft accident investigators in discussing how an otherwise well-qualified and competent pilot could allow a perfectly good airplane to crash: "loss of situation awareness." It adequately describes a complex situation which has so many changing variables and messages that the ability to deal with the "big picture" is virtually impossible because the pilot has been overwhelmed and has effectively lost control of the situation and therefore the plane.

Three days later, I read in the *New York Times* that on June 18, SECNAV had turned over the entire Tailhook investigation to the DoD IG.[17] He asked the office to review and comment on the NIS and IG investigations and also to provide its own independent analysis of what went on in Las Vegas. "Criticisms of the investigations, along with rumor and innuendo of cover-up, have eroded seriously the Department of the Navy's credibility to further the Tailhook '91 matter" is what Garret had written in his released memo. By shifting the responsibility up the chain of command, he effectively ended the further participation of NIS and IG and gave all responsibility to the organization led by Derek J. Vander Schaaf, the acting Pentagon inspector general.

A few days later on Sunday evening, June 21, I flew my next all-nighter trip from Dulles to London's Heathrow landing there at 9:00 AM Monday morning. Along with most of my buddies in Annapolis, I had become a great fan of author Patrick O'Brian and had read all of his *Aubrey-Maturin Series* novels. Whenever I had a London layover, I would try to visit at least one of the nautical sites described in his books or some other place of military significance. This visit, my objective was the city of Portsmouth. I had tried to talk my captain and fellow copilot into joining me, but they agreed that catching up on a missed night's sleep was a more prudent use of their time.

After I got to my hotel room, I got out of my uniform, took a quick shower, changed clothes, and took the "tube" to London Waterloo where I changed trains for the one-hour-forty-five-minute ride to Portsmouth Harbor Train Station. Fortunately, I met a fellow history buff who was also travelling to Portsmouth. He agreed to wake me up when we arrived as I kept dozing off and feared I'd miss my stop.

We arrived around noon, and before entering the nautical museum area, I grabbed a bite to eat and had a beer. I spent the afternoon taking in the various exhibits. All were interesting, but I devoted more time, by far, walking the decks of HMS *Victory*, the famous flagship of Lord Nelson. As the hero of the Battle of Trafalgar in 1805, Nelson decisively defeated the French fleet but had been shot during the engagement by a French sharpshooter. He was taken below deck and perished in the arms of Capt. Hardy. That scene is accurately depicted on the *Victory*. It was a fascinating look at history which brought life to O'Brian's stories of Capt. Jack Aubrey and his companion, Dr. Stephen Maturin.

Having successfully journeyed back to London, I went directly to my favorite pub just a few blocks walk from my hotel off Hyde Park. After a few pints and some fish and chips, I was more than ready for a long good night's sleep before flying back to Dulles the next morning.

Now back in Annapolis on the night of June 23, I was somewhat relieved to learn that I hadn't missed any major news or announcements while on my trip to England. Perhaps, I had overestimated the anti-Navy mood in Washington and the influence of the fourth estate. Unfortunately, all that changed the next day: Wednesday, June 24.

After returning from my hour-long morning bike ride, I showered and went to breakfast at the 912 Squadron. As sometimes happens, Luke and I were the only members present. We chatted about our recent airline trips and were in conversations about Tailhook when Bill, the owner, came over and gave us a copy of the Washington Post. There on the front page was a picture of a bewildered Lt. Paula Coughlin under a headline which read "A Gauntlet of Terror, Frustration—Navy Pilot Recounts Tailhook Incident" by John Lancaster.[18]

I put down my breakfast sandwich and immediately began to read the article.

"Holy shit," I said to Luke after I finished. "Naval Aviation is screwed—big time. This one is going to send everyone into orbit." Before saying anything else, I asked him to read it while I went back to finishing my meal.

A few minutes later, Luke put the paper down, looked up at me, and said, "I'm sure glad I'm not in the Navy. Just when you hoped things might settle down along comes this. This article certainly puts a sympathetic face on Tailhook that will drive both sides crazy." I agreed wholeheartedly with his assessment and tried to imagine what the immediate reactions would be. As Luke had chores to do, he left me alone at the table.

A few minutes later, Bill came over and sat down. "I read the article before I opened up this morning. Pretty bad, isn't it?" he asked.

"I'm afraid, in this case, the light at the end of the tunnel is a bad-ass locomotive and it's going to be extremely destructive ," I said. The feelings I was now experiencing were very similar to those I had back in October. This was going to be horrible. Little did I know how much worse it would become a mere eight hours later when, according to the article, Lt. Coughlin was to appear on a major TV news program.

I was out all day and had returned to my home just in time to watch *ABC World News Tonight* with Peter Jennings. Ever since Walter Cronkite retired from CBS, it had become my favorite news program. I had just sat down after getting a beer from my refrigerator when I saw her—Lt. Paula Coughlin, in uniform, being interviewed by Mr. Jennings. I could hardly believe my eyes, but there she was, explaining all the graphic details of her Tailhook assault. As shocking as it had been to read her story in print earlier in the day, it was exponentially worse watching it live.[19]

After the interview was completed, I was emotionally drained. There was nothing I could say and there was no one I wished to talk to, so I took the phone off the hook. I just sat there in silence for a while trying to make some sense out of all this. I came up with nothing, so I decided to take a walk to the dock at my waterfront complex. Gazing out on the beautiful Severn River and Chesapeake Bay had always put me in a better mood, but tonight was different. The magical calming effect wasn't quite working. Time to visit McGarvey's—surely that will work!

A few hours later, I returned home from the saloon. It had been a quiet night: neither Mike nor any of my crowd was there, so I just sat at the bar and had my usual dinner accompanied by a few Aviator brews. Guido, my friendly bartender, and I chatted mostly about our favorite team, the Yankees, and their recent performances.

Before retiring to my upstairs bedroom, I checked my answering machine. As I had predicted, there were a couple of messages from my 912 buddies commenting about the Coughlin interview. There was also one that I found very curious. It was just a very short message telling me that "earlier today, the DoD IG had instructed the NIS and Navy IG to cease all investigations effective immediately." No name was left, and I didn't recognize the male voice.

Next evening, I watched as Peter Jennings concluded his two-part interview of Lt. Coughlin. I had to admit that it was very well done. It seemed to be factual and unemotional. Of course, it only gave her side of the story, but it was a powerful and convincing performance—certainly, it would be difficult to refute or mitigate her assertions. Some of us might call it "piling on," because the next evening on ABC's *Primetime*, Sam Donaldson had another exclusive about Tailhook. It featured several female victims and Sen. John Warner and Adm. Kelso. It was a devastating piece of journalism.[20]

Of all the naval aviators who had also watched the Jenning's interview and were affected by Lt. Coughlin's interviews, none was more powerful than the nation's Commander in Chief, President George H. W. Bush. He had read about and seen the interviews and was reportedly "so moved" by her story that he invited her to the White House on June 26. He and his wife, Barbara, met with her for tea and "expressed their sympathy and assured her that there would be a full investigation," a White House spokesman had said.[21] In fact, the president "wept when he heard Lt. Coughlin recount how she was forced through the gauntlet of two hundred very drunken men who happened to be her comrades and peers."[22]

This wasn't the only Friday meeting which the president had about Tailhook. Earlier in the morning, he received a full briefing of all aspects of the affair and its aftermath at the White House from SECDEF Cheney. Not long after, SECNAV Garrett delivered his resignation letter to Cheney at his Pentagon office—this time, he had accepted it.

In his resignation letter to the president, Sec. Garrett accepted "full responsibility," adding, "I hold myself accountable for the leadership failure which allowed the egregious conduct at Tailhook to occur in the first place."[23]

It was not all that surprising to learn that President Bush merely "accepted" the secretary's resignation.

There would be no words of praise, no ceremonies, and no awards for this former naval flight officer—the third high-ranking Navy official to have his career ended by his attendance at Tailhook. The big question: Who or what was next?

DoD IG Report: Part 1

"We will not see one successful court-martial come out of this process."

IT DIDN'T TAKE LONG FOR either question to be answered. The new acting Secretary of the Navy, Dan Howard, made his mark on July 1, just five days after his former boss, Larry Garrett, was forced to step down. He had summoned three hundred of the top Navy and Marine Corps leadership to attend his personal briefing in the Pentagon auditorium. Complete details of his speech, including the videotape, were given to the press a couple of days later so that the initial rumor that he was angry and upset were confirmed. Howard had told the assembled group that "it is important to underline the fact that what had happened at Tailhook was not just a problem with the integration of men and women in our ranks…It was just as much a problem with the toleration of Stone Age attitudes about warriors returning from the sea, about Navy and Marine Corps people who think the rules of civility and common decency can be suspended at will, about alcohol as an excuse for disgraceful behavior."[24]

He announced several initiatives, one of which was extremely controversial and was sure to upset the Naval Aviation community: he called for the disbandment of the Tailhook Association. He also published an ALNAV (a memo to be distributed to all Navy and Marine Corps personnel) which addressed the issues of sexual harassment and standards of conduct of service men and women. He directed that all commands "stand down" for a day for mandatory training of these two issues.[25] Viewing the videotape of Howard's address, showing the Navy CNO and Marine Corps Commandant at his side, was to be part of the training session.

Just before going to bed on the same evening when I learned about SECNAV's performance in the Pentagon auditorium, I answered my phone. It was a close Navy buddy calling from the San Diego area. Like me, he was an active drilling reservist who was also a United pilot. He asked if I had heard the latest out of NAS Miramar (aka Fightertown USA). When I answered that I hadn't heard anything of late, he spent the next ten minutes describing two recent "Tomcat Follies" skits performed at the Miramar Officers' Club by members of F-14 Fighter Squadrons based there.

After he finished, I told him I had no idea that "follies" were still being performed anywhere since I hadn't heard or talked about them since my days on the *Ranger* back in '71. I was even more surprised to learn that they were being performed stateside at naval air stations. I had believed that they were only done aboard carriers. But the larger issue was the performance itself and more importantly who was the target of skits. In this case, the target was none other than Rep. Patricia Schroeder, Democrat, Colorado.

As a member of the House Armed Services Committee, she was a powerful and vocal critic of the Defense Department's policies regarding women in the military. Seen by many JOs in the Naval Aviation community as the "enemy," it would not be surprising to learn that she might be the target of opportunity of one of their skits. But recalling the several follies' skits in which I participated or witnessed aboard the *Saratoga* or *Ranger* in the '60s and early '70s, I found it inconceivable that in this day and age of "PC" how anything like those could be performed "in public." But, indeed, they had been in mid-June at Miramar and were about to make news nationwide. Rep. Schroeder was the punch line of two segments: "Hickory, Dickory, Dock, Pat Schroeder can suck my cock!" was performed by the Screaming Eagles of VF-51 commanded by Cdr. David Tyler.

Another skit, whose final line was "Pat, don't be a dick!" was done by VF-111, commanded by Cdr. Robert Clement.[26]

Both officers were first relieved of their commands by Vice Adm. Ruddy Kohn, Commander, Naval Air Forces Pacific, who would relieve a total of five officers of their commands and punish eighteen others.(Subsequently, both were permanently relieved by Adm. Robert J. Kelly, Commander, Pacific Fleet.)[27] Coincidentally, ADM Kohn, had been my Operations officer boss back in '71–'73 at NAS Lemoore when I was an instructor pilot and LSO in VA-122. He and I had met briefly and exchanged hellos after the flag panel at Tailhook'91 where he had been on stage with ADM Dunleavy. Clearly, Naval Aviation would continue make front-page news.

On July 7, Secretary of Defense Cheney announced that he was naming, for a 120-day term, thirty-six-year-old Mr. Sean O'Keefe as the acting secretary of the Navy. Since Senate approval would not be required, this unusual step removed the possibility that there would be a long and contentious Senate fight to confirm his nomination in the midst of the presidential election. O'Keefe, a Cheney confidant, had been the Pentagon's controller and had replaced Howard who was seen by many as too closely associated with the Tailhook affair and especially the lack of leadership which allowed it and subsequently was having great difficulty addressing it.[28]

Two days later, Sec. O'Keefe issued a memorandum to the Navy CNO and Marine Corps Commandant in which he gave his complete support to the ongoing DoD IG investigation. "I expect full cooperation with this effort by all uniformed members and civilian employees of the Department of the Navy…In particular, every effort should be made on an individual basis to cooperate fully with the DoD IG's oral interviews into this matter." He concluded by advising that "anyone with information relevant to the DoD IG investigation should be encouraged to call the DoD IG hotline number."[29]

CNO Kelso then forwarded that memo to the commander in chief, Atlantic and Pacific Fleets, the chief of the Naval Education and Training, and the chief of the Naval Reserve as an attachment to his own Tailhook memo. His reiterated that "disciplinary actions or further inquiries related to Tailhook '91 be held in abeyance until otherwise notified." He further directed that those four commands ensure that the DoD IG is "provided unrestricted access to all records, files, and other data considered relevant to the inquiry and...every effort should be made on an individual basis to cooperate fully with the DoD IG's oral interviews into the matter."[30]

Clearly, the DoD IG was now the only game in town. Normally, this organization dealt with issues like fraud, waste, and abuse and other white-collar crimes as most of their investigations were, in fact, audits. But within that organization was another group that was assigned the task of prosecuting those responsible for criminal activities at Tailhook: the DCIS, the Defense Criminal Investigation Service.

During the next two months, we were treated to a period of calmness since there were, thankfully, few headline stories about new allegations or revelations. There were, however, an increased number of scuttlebutt tales circulating about DoD IG special agents conducting their investigations. Many of them had descended on squadrons and air wings based stateside at naval air stations and deployed overseas on aircraft carriers. *Much more aggressive* and *hell bent on prosecutions* were phrases often heard in these stories which were making the rounds.

The relative quiet ended on the morning of September 24 with published articles appearing in many of the top newspapers concerning the release of the DoD IG Report Part 1 later the same day.[31] These columns had obviously been written after the authors had been given the actual report .They accurately forecast what Sec. O'Keefe would do and say later at his afternoon Pentagon press conference.[32]

"The Report of Investigation: Tailhook '91, Part 1, Review of the Navy Investigations" was a thirty-two-page memorandum, with eleven enclosures, for the acting secretary of the Navy from the deputy inspector general.[33] As directed by former SECNAV Larry Garrett, it addressed the two Navy investigations. If the highest-ranking Navy officials within the secretariat, IG, NIS, and JAG organizations had earlier believed that the DoD IG had come to their rescue, they were surely disappointed. In fact, they must have been outraged by the substance and tone expressed. The Report was highly critical of all the leaders involved in both Navy investigations save Sec. Barbara Pope.

Its recommendations to the acting SECNAV included not only the removal of the undersecretary, the JAG, the Commander NIS, and the Navy IG but taking "appropriate disciplinary action with respect to the JAG and Commander NIS for their failure to fulfill their professional responsibilities." Not surprisingly, former SECNAV Garrett did not escape intense scrutiny. DoD investigators interviewed several witnesses who dramatically contradicted Garrett's sworn testimony regarding his activities with respect to his visits to some of the third-floor hospitality suites. In an August 20 phone conversation with Michael Suessman, the assistant inspector general, Garrett had been invited "to submit to a polygraph examination… to resolve the apparent conflict between my sworn statement and the testimony of others." On August 25, he responded by letter (an enclosure in the report) declining Suessman's invitation. "My word is my bond, always has been, and always will be, and I am deeply offended by the suggestion that a polygraph examination is required to somehow corroborate that I told the truth as I know it."[34]

Even though Vander Schaaf's memo was dated September 21, I personally thought Sec. O'Keefe must have had more than just three days to consider how he would respond to the report. He delivered his fifteen-minute statement at noon on the twenty-fourth addressing both the conclusions and recommendations in great detail.[35]

Most notably, he announced the retirements of Admirals Williams (NIS) and Gordon (JAG) effective November 1 and the anticipated replacement of Davis (NIG) after a more senior admiral received Senate confirmation. He concluded that Undersecretary Howard had been ill-served by and received bad advice from his naval officer subordinates but would remain in his present position. Additionally, the head of NIS would henceforth be a civilian appointee and the Navy IG would be elevated to a three-star rank who would be retired after his IG tour of duty.

Apart from these personnel issues, he emphasized that, speaking for the Navy leadership, "We get it." He described the recent steps the Navy had taken to implement an aggressive campaign to address the cultural problem which has allowed "demeaning behavior and attitudes toward women to exist within the Navy Department." He couldn't anticipate when "Part 2" of the report dealing with criminal and inappropriate behavior at Tailhook would be issued but reassured everyone that "appropriate action" would be taken when he received it.

As I watched the hour-long press conference on C-Span,[36] I couldn't help but imagine how I would have responded to the penetrating and accusatory questions asked by various members of the press. Sec. O'Keefe, I thought, was both skillful and adroit in talking about Undersecretary Howard, his predecessor, Garrett, and Admirals Williams, Gordon, and Davis. Responding to one inquiry, he said that the entire episode could be characterized as "a failure of process aggravated by a failure of individuals."

I was especially interested when he talked about the retirement of Williams and Gordon. He said that "their retirements were encouraged and they submitted them and they were guided by their consciences." The distinct impression was that they had been fired. I wondered if this, in fact, had been the case for my former USNA '64 upperclassman and Seventeenth Company shipmate, Ted Gordon.

Although not close at school, I had several friendly social and professional engagements with Ted while he served on Secretary of the Navy John Lehman's staff in the 1980s.

Assistant Secretary of Defense for Public Affairs Pete Williams (now an NBC News TV correspondent) followed O'Keefe, and he, too, received several questions about the report and Sec. Cheney's reaction to it. In sum, Williams said that Cheney had been fully briefed and completely supported all the actions which O'Keefe had proposed in responding to the report's recommendations. He had "complete confidence" that O'Keefe would provide the necessary leadership to address the Navy's problems.

At least for now, it appeared to me that the emphasis of the press, as well as the Navy itself, had taken dead aim on the five principals: Undersec. Howard, Asst. Sec. Pope, Adm. Williams (NIS), Adm. Davis (NIG), and Adm. Gordon (JAG), who all had significant roles in the conduct of the two Navy investigations. It was very apparent that O'Keefe accepted, as fact, the report's conclusions and had quickly enacted its personnel and organizational change recommendations without input from that group who had been so thoroughly pilloried by the DoD IG.

The next morning, as I was cleaning up after returning from an early-morning workout, I answered my phone. It was an Annapolis friend who told me to turn on the TV to the *Today Show.* After I did, I saw Sec. O'Keefe talking about the report and the actions which he had initiated to help solve the Navy's problems. I thought he had gone out of his way to lay almost complete blame on Admirals Gordon, Williams, and Davis for the shortcomings and inadequacies described in the report. But as I later found out, he wasn't the only Navy official making news before the TV cameras.

Admirals Davis, Gordon, and Williams had been given the DoD IG report on Wednesday night, just eighteen hours before O'Keefe's press conference. On Friday, the Navy's general counsel, Craig King, had sent all the principals a memo affording each the opportunity to respond. JAG Adm. Gordon was the first to respond. He immediately authored a two-page rebuttal to the report, which he distributed to various news organizations. He followed that up with an appearance on CNN that evening. From my own point of view, I think his arguments cast serious doubt on the accuracy and validity of the report's conclusions and therefore its recommendations.

One of Adm. Williams's first requests after getting the general counsel's memo was to request from the DoD IG the background material which was the basis for their conclusions regarding his participation. Quite astonishingly, he was instructed to seek these documents by initiating a FOIA request. (Note: Despite two attempts, documents were never provided).

All the principals eventually provided voluminous responses to SECNAV O'Keefe. On October 22, barely a month after receiving the report, he sent a two-hundred-page rebuttal, which contained a five-page blistering critique to Vander Schaaf, the DoD IG. He convincingly argued, based on his principals' submissions, that there now exists "serious questions about the IG's fairness...content...and judgment."

Those submissions included words like deceitful, vindictive, unfair, abusive, and fallacious to describe the DoD IG investigation and tactics. Incredibly, to me at least, O'Keefe nevertheless agreed with the DoD IG's conclusion that the Navy leadership was at fault in not producing a Tailhook report that was useful and thorough. "The written comments of the four individuals are not sufficient to absolve them of some measure of responsibility for this failure."

Fortunately for Gordon and Williams, there was one area where there was significant disagreement. O'Keefe did not accept Vander Schaaf's recommendation that he take additional disciplinary measures against Gordon and Williams: their impending November 1 retirements would thus end their official involvement.

Though not very relevant to the central thrust of O'Keefe's response was a very interesting and astonishing revelation, which was contained in the submission by Undersecretary Dan Howard. He admitted that he had purposely disobeyed SECNAV Garrett's instruction and had prematurely released the NIS and NIG reports in April. He said that "it was my motive to embarrass the Navy as much as possible" since he believed that taking this action was needed to get everyone's attention. Interestingly, had the reports not been released until their known inadequacies had been remedied, things might have turned out far differently.

Months later, I learned many more details about the conduct and aftermath of the Navy IG and NIS investigations from two of the principals: now retired Admirals Gordon and Williams. Each had given sit-down interviews to Capt. J. Robert Lunny, JAGC, USNR (Ret.) and later published in the *Naval Reserve Association News* in January and February 1992, respectively.[37, 38]

In an article titled "Tailhook—The Other Side," Gordon wasted no time in blaming the "civilian political leadership of the Navy" for the debacle. "They took charge of this investigation and began to deal with what is a good order and discipline problem outside the well-tested institutions of the Navy...during the presidential election year, the entire focus turned to satisfying the demands of the press and avoidance of embarrassment to the political administration instead of on the Navy and Marine Corps' critical need for good order and discipline." The result was foreseeable: "it is a very bad situation turning into a tragic one."

In the five-page interview, Gordon gave his take on the two Navy investigations which he felt would have been sufficient to address the problems had they not been short-circuited by the decisions of his civilian bosses. He argued the inquiries were just beginning to get to those responsible when they were halted. His harshest comments though were directed at the DoD IG and the acting SECNAV. The DoD IG "doesn't understand the role of the JAG...and invented one...and then concluded that I didn't fulfill that invented one." He was particularly offended by O'Keefe's remarks about his "forced" retirement. Months earlier, Gordon had planned to retire effective November 1 and had submitted the papers "well in advance of the *DoD IG Report*," but O'Keefe had never publically acknowledged this fact. Instead, he allowed the perception that Gordon had been summarily retired to continue.

The former JAG's concluding remarks were indeed prescient. Asked his thoughts about "Part 2," he opined that it would be no better than "Part 1." "Political outcome not facts" are what are driving the DoD IG. "I truly believe that the command influence problem created by our political leadership is so severe that we will not see one successful court-martial come out of this process."

In his interview with Reserve's Capt. Lunney, Adm. Williams expanded on his reply to the DoD IG report, which he had sent to O'Keefe on October 6, two weeks after he had first seen the report. "I believe that the report itself and the manner in which it was handled violated all of the rules people in this country associate with fundamental fairness."

He strongly argued that before the DoD IG took over the investigation in June, the Navy's chain of command was quite capable of handling the ten known cases referred by the NIS as well as the thirty-three cases by the NIG: seventeen of which involved squadron commanding officers who were in charge of the third-floor hospitality suites. He also believed that more cases would have resulted from further NIS investigations had they not been called off.

He vehemently defended himself against the charges made in the report concerning his supposed comments about women in the Navy. He categorically denied making the highly inflammatory statements about "female Navy pilots being go-go dancers, topless dancers, and hookers," which were attributed to him by Sec. Pope. He cited numerous examples of the DoD IG's failure "to use even the most basic investigative techniques to ascertain the conclusions which they reached."

Contained in his interview were two related themes which were deeply disturbing. The first was William's firmly held belief that all of the principals "had not been afforded the basic protections of due process and had been criticized unfairly by the DoD IG." The second was that the "evidentiary standards underlying the information in the *DoD IG Report* and the standards of proof required to support their conclusions" were put into serious question by SECNAV in his rebuttal.

Taken together, these statements by the former JAG and commander of the NIS created a great deal of fear and anxiety in me, and I was certain, in every naval aviator even remotely connected to Tailhook '91. Here we learned from two top Navy leaders that they and others had been screwed badly by a corrupted system that had its own rules and seemed to be concerned not with facts but solely political expedience. "Holy shit," I said to myself, "if our top-ranking leaders could be treated with this degree of injustice, imagine how all us underlings will make out in the process."

DoD IG Report: Part 2

"The facts have been discovered, and justice will be served."

ON TUESDAY, NOVEMBER 3, 1992, Bill Clinton received a plurality in the popular vote and a wide Electoral College margin over his opponent, President George H. W. Bush, in winning the presidential race. One election consequence of particular concern to the Navy establishment was that there would necessarily be a complete change of civilian leadership, which would have to deal with "Part 2" of the DoD IG report.

Historians generally agree that the Navy's political power in Washington, DC, had reached its zenith at the end of and immediately following World War II. It could claim that President Roosevelt had been a Navy assistant secretary, Secretary of Defense Forrestal had just previously been the Navy secretary and President Roosevelt's chief of staff was Adm. Leahy. However, the power and influence changed significantly by the time President Truman signed the National Security Act in July 1947 and its amendments in 1949. There had been a dramatic changing of the guard (and power) from the Navy to the Army. President Truman and his Secretary of Defense, Louis Johnson, had been Army officers in WWI, and his chief of staff was Gen. Eisenhower, a five-star general. Truman's armed services "unification" plan, contained in the act, established primacy of the

Defense Department over the Navy, Army and the newly formed Air Force departments. The act changed many things, which lessened the Navy's importance including the elimination of secretary of the Navy as a cabinet post, which it had been since its inception in 1798.

The gradual diminution of its role and influence continued until February 5, 1981, when my occasional sailing mate, John Lehman, was confirmed as President Reagan's secretary of the Navy. The young but experienced secretary of the Navy wasted little time in becoming a most vocal and successful proponent of the nation's *Maritime Strategy*. Not since another previous Secretary of the Navy, Theodore Roosevelt, adopted Adm. Alfred Thayer Mahan's principles of sea power had there been such an articulate and influential spokesman for a large and powerful "blue ocean" Navy. Who would President-elect Clinton choose to fill this important position as secretary was a question on the minds of many Navy personnel.

However, who would be the secretary of the Navy's immediate boss was announced on December 17, 1992, when Rep. Leslie Aspin, chairman of the House Armed Services Committee, was chosen to be the incoming secretary of Defense. Shortly after the new president took his oath of office on January 20, 1993, the Senate unanimously approved Aspin who was sworn in the next day as secretary of Defense. A secretary of Navy still had not been named, but in a most unusual move, the new administration named the CNO, Adm. Kelso, the acting secretary of the Navy, thus double-hatting him. It was a move without precedence in the Navy's 217-year history. Several days after the presidential inauguration, Vice Adm. J. Paul D. Reason, commander, Atlantic Fleet Surface Force (SURFLANT), was chosen by Adm. Kelso to be the Navy's CDA (Consolidated Disposition Authority). As such, he would serve as the head naval officer for all Navy Tailhook-related cases. He was an Academy grad class of 1965 who had a distinguished career as a Black Shoe—a ship driver. He was the first African-American to attain three-stars in the Navy and had once served as naval aide to President Jimmy Carter. While the choice of establishing a CDA by former Secretary of Navy O'Keefe was controversial for a number of reasons, the choice of

Adm. Reason was well received as most thought him to be a straight shooter with no agenda other than doing the best job possible.

His Marine Corps equivalent as CDA was Lt. Gen. Charles C. Krulak, USMC—a USNA '64 classmate of Adm. Ted Gordon. The son of a Lt. Gen. USMC, born in Quantico, VA., he was a much decorated "grunt" in Vietnam having been awarded the Silver Star, three Bronze Stars, and two Purple Hearts. I still had vivid memories of him dating back to several very early-morning exhaustive PT workouts which he led during my plebe summer. "He bleeds green" is what I heard about him. "Tough" is how I remember him and that's how many described him thirty-one years later!

In early February, I had heard rumors and leaks from "well-informed Pentagon sources" that "Part 2" of the IG report had essentially been completed and was ready for publication. Indeed, fifteen congresswomen, in a February 22 letter, urged Secretary of Defense Aspin "to release the report immediately, instead of waiting until a civilian secretary is in place."[39] However, it was apparent that Aspin was not going to reverse his stated February 16 position that he would wait until after a nominee was to be named. The reasoning was sound: it needed to be given to someone other than Adm. Kelso who had attended Tailhook. Finally, on April 21, President Clinton announced his intention to name John H. Dalton, another personally familiar USNA grad, to be secretary of the Navy.

Two days later, the proverbial "shit hit the fan" for it was on that Black Friday when Secretary of Defense Aspin transmitted the report to the Navy, which immediately released it to the public.[40] At an afternoon Pentagon press conference packed with media representatives, the CNO, Adm. Kelso, and the Marine Corps Commandant, Gen. Mundy, each delivered a prepared statement about the report and then answered several questions.[41]

Adm. Kelso reaffirmed that Vice Adm. Reason had been chosen to handle "administrative or disciplinary actions that come out of this report." He also noted the reasons why this procedure would guarantee fairness and efficiency. Gen. Mundy likewise announced Lt. Gen. Krulak was chosen for the Marine Corps cases.

Kelso listed all the changes that have or would shortly come about in the Navy to ensure that "our people uphold the highest standards of behavior across the board...we have moved out to fix the problem." The CNO assured everyone that in the end, "the facts have been discovered and justice will be served."

In his released statement about the report, Aspin said Dalton would be kept informed about Tailhook issues. The DoD IG investigative files or cases in which there was sexual misconduct or other improper activity by individuals would be conveyed to Adm. Reason or Gen. Krulak. On the other hand, there was another section of the report which contained the cases of admirals and generals who had attended Tailhook. This file would remain with Aspin until Sec. Dalton was confirmed at which time he would transmit it to him.

The "Report" itself was shocking and devastating.[42] The one-page memorandum for the Secretary of Defense was dated April 12 from Deputy Inspector General Vander Schaaf and noted that "misconduct at the 1991 Tailhook Symposium was more widespread than previously reported by the Navy...ninety victims of indecent assault and a significant number of incidents of indecent exposure, sexual misconduct, and other improprieties...fifty officers made false statements....more than 140 officer files are being referred to for appropriate action. The files of thirty Navy admirals, two Marine Corps generals, and three Navy Reserve admirals will eventually be turned over to the new secretary of the Navy."

Reading just this transmittal letter got my blood pressure to rise. Next came the "Foreword," which really put me into a high state of anxiety. It described the report, as I interpreted the words, as a no-holds-barred exposé using the most intimate and sexually graphic words and pictures they could find. Its last paragraph, "commending all those aviators not associated with Tailhook and hoping that their morale won't suffer," I found to be laughable!

The two-page "Executive Summary," I believe, purposely painted the picture that Tailhook '91 was a combination of organized mayhem, criminal behavior, a wild frat house party, bachelor party, and bacchanalian "free fire zone" where everyone either participated in or knew about or condoned all these activities.

I then read the two pages of contents, which included Section VI Indecent Assaults: (A) Gauntlet, (B) Victims, and (C) Other Assaults and Injuries; Section VII Indecent Exposure: (A) Streaking, (B) Mooning, and (C) "Ballwalking"; Other Improper Activity: (A) Leg Shaving, (B) "Belly/Navel Shots," (C) Pornographic, (D) Chicken Fights (E) "Butt Biting," (F) "Zapping," and (G) Public and Paid Sex.

"Oh my god, this is going to be a disaster," I said to myself.

I then skipped the next two sections and read and then reread the "Conclusions." My take was that the report indicated the aviators who participated in any of the various assaults, exposures, or improper activities and those who witnessed them and those who knew about them all shared equally in the blame. All those COs and "flags" knew or should have known bear responsibility as well. To me, the IG was telling everyone there is a much larger problem than anyone could have known. His message was clear: "Now, Navy, go out and prosecute all those we've identified because they are guilty as charged."

I then made a decision not to read any more of the report until I had time to digest and make sense of that which I had already read. Besides, my head was throbbing. I got back to my home late afternoon from my Friday "Navy Reserve day" at the IG office in the Navy Yard. After a forty-five-minute hill climb routine on my Life Cycle bicycle, I showered, put on some casual clothes, grabbed a beer, and watched ABC news. There was a segment covering the Tailhook report and Adm. Kelso's and Gen. Mundy's press conference. After watching the piece, my headache returned in spades.

It was time to go to McGarvey's.

Most of my friends who were at the saloon had not seen TV news that evening, so they weren't aware of the Tailhook story. It was a blessing because I really didn't want to think or talk about it—there would be plenty of time in the coming days after the press and the politicians got hold of this.

Tonight would be shared with my buddies—shooting the bull about many issues—flying, women, good times, motorcycling, and sailing, to name a few of our favorite topics. The place got packed, and Mike, Luke, Fred, and I had a ball. Several hours later, around 1:00 AM, I had consumed my last "one for the ditch" and decided it was time to call it an evening.

I awoke early, fixed coffee, gathered the report, and sat down at my desk. I was determined to read through the seven sections of the report totaling more than seventy pages which I had skipped the day before. Before I did, I read Saturday morning's *Washington Post*'s front page article on the Tailhook report by John Lancaster: "Tailhook Probe Implicates 140 Officers."[43] All things considered, I thought it to be a pretty subdued critique of the report.

I then began to read the remainder of "Part 2." The nine-page section describing the twenty-two third-floor Hilton hospitality suites included diagrams, pictures, detailed and graphic descriptions of horrible behavior, descriptions and costs of damages, and types and amounts of alcohol dispensed, numbers and types of assaults, and other "improper" behavior. Reading this section and scanning its accompanying and far more detailed sixty-page "Appendix E: Individual Squadron Suite Summaries" left me awestruck and bewildered.

The next seventeen-page section addressed "Indecent Assaults." The first twelve pages described the gauntlet in the most shocking and graphic detail and summarized the assaults on ninety victims. Its fifty-four-page companion, "Appendix F," described, in the most intimate detail, the actual assaults. All cases referred to each victim by number only but there were a few exceptions—one of them was "Victim Number 50": Lt. Paula Coughlin.

I could hardly believe the level of detail in all the individual stories. After reading a few, it became increasingly difficult to continue because they were repetitive in using so many tantalizing and salacious details. After I had finished, my head wanted to explode. I was having a difficult time separating the utter contempt I had for the investigators with the outrage I had for my fellow aviators who were the perpetrators of the assaults.

I had been at the report for more than two and a half hours and was mentally and emotionally drained and also very hungry. It was just after 9:00 AM, so I knew if I hurried, I would only be a few minutes late for breakfast with the "boys" of the 912 Squadron at Jim's Corner. I jumped on my Low Rider and made it to our hangout in less than ten minutes.

Fortunately, several of my 912 friends were already there, and as I had guessed, everyone had either seen reports on TV or read about the Tailhook report in the papers. As always, the conversation was animated, intense, and highly critical of the DoD investigators. The only time where consensus was achieved was when we all agreed that life in many of the carrier-based squadrons must be crazy. When we talked about the numbers of aviators indicted and all the flags in jeopardy, it was hard to believe Tailhook '91 had evolved into such an incredible "Charlie Foxtrot."

After a couple of hours, I returned home and immediately resumed reading the report. Section VII "Indecent Exposure" and Section VIII "Other Improper Activity" were five and eight pages, respectively. Graphic word descriptions, as well as photos, were included in defining and discussing these items.

The next section contained four pages describing the security which the Hilton and the Tailhook Association had provided. "Officer Attitudes and Leadership" was the penultimate section of ten pages. I experienced an increasing level of angst as I read the three pages that talked about the flag officers who had attended the event. I found it noteworthy that SECDEF would continue to "hold" that portion of the report addressing the thirty-five admirals and generals to himself until after John Dalton, the new secretary of the Navy, had received Senate confirmation at which time he would deliver it to him.

I spent some time decompressing while I contemplated all which I had read. Trying to square the report's version of Tailhook with what I had personally witnessed eighteen months before was an impossible chore. Some things really confused me. While I had only been to three previous Tailhooks—and none since 1984—I had absolutely no knowledge of the gauntlet. I could not believe that any of the various assaults described in the report were knowingly perpetrated by naval aviators. Everything I had ever seen was the same type of prank and "Animal House" behavior which took place at spring break functions in Ft. Lauderdale, Cozumel, and Daytona. As a grown man, I had witnessed very many "colorful" examples of adult behavior at Mardi Gras, and I had been to a good number of bachelor parties but could never remember behavior which I thought was criminal. Certainly, there had been many in poor or boorish taste but none which constituted a law-breaking offense.

The totality of the report convinced me it was reasonable to believe that some aviators had crossed the line and had deliberately participated in assaults. However, it seemed that the inspector general had combined those criminal activities with all those consensual, adult-type behaviors. Thus, he was now condemning not just the criminals but everyone who either took part or who had witnessed the type behavior which he now judged to be indecent, improper, or inappropriate. Lastly, I felt he also took direct aim at the flags and held them responsible. Even if they hadn't seen anything, they ought to have known "stuff" was happening based on their seniority and experience. He seemed to argue that they should have done something to stop all this bad behavior based on mere "intuition."

Just when I thought all was lost, I happened to scan the table of contents and noticed two interesting titles: "Tailhook Association Submittal" and "Navy Submittal." They were Appendices labeled B and C and provided some comic relief, although, I'm certain, that wasn't their intended purpose. They were six-page and two-page summaries of how the respective organizations described the symposium. Both described it as accurately as if I had authored the summarizations. Both described it in glowing terms as being the "best ever." The problem was that neither spoke of "Tailhook—The Other Story," which the IG had written about in its report. No doubt, both organizations' attorneys had censored it so that there was no mention of anything even close to being considered "inappropriate." Chuckling to myself, I was reminded of one of my favorite military books, *Catch-22*.

Over the next two weeks, it came as a surprise to no one that Naval Aviation and Tailhook were at the receiving end of so many scathing articles, commentaries, and editorials that if this were a football game, "piling on" penalties would have been constantly assessed.

Unfortunately, this was a Washington story full of sex, alcohol, and men portrayed in films by Robert Duvall in *The Great Santini* and Tom Cruise in *Top Gun*. There would be no stopping this feeding frenzy.

While Tailhook and the contents of the "Report" continued to be the subject of so much press and discussion, the real action had already begun in early February. In Quantico and Norfolk, Gen. Krulak and Adm. Reason were kept busy organizing their staffs and developing appropriate procedures to deal with their new responsibilities as CDA's.

Adm. Reason depended primarily upon his SURFLANT staff judge advocate, Capt. Jeffrey Williams. He was assisted by Capt. Edward Ellis, the head of the Norfolk Navy Legal Services Office (NLSO), to lead this effort into unchartered waters. Because there were many players with different and, quite often, competing agendas involved in this effort, it soon evolved into a difficult and painstaking operation. In late February, DoD IG investigators finally delivered case files on 117 individuals to Reason's Norfolk office where they continued to be actively involved in "their" cases.

A team of Navy JAG officers, approved by Reason, had been formed to review and analyze each of the cases. They then made recommendations regarding appropriate dispositions to another group of senior naval line officers who been approved by Reason. After being briefed, they then discussed the cases and then submitted their recommendations on each case to Adm. Reason who would ultimately decide how to proceed.

There were essentially four courses of action which could be chosen: (1) drop the case, (2) require further investigation, (3) admiral's mast, and (4) court-martial. Generally speaking, nonjudicial punishment (NJP) is administered by an admiral during admiral's mast in an informal setting (i.e., the admiral's office) for minor offenses but can include fairly severe monetary and/or administrative career-ending penalties. On the other hand, a court-martial is a far more formal and time-consuming procedure for major offenses, which, in the case of an officer, normally involves a JAG judge, a jury, attorneys, etc.

The case review process had dragged on for months for a number of reasons not the least of which was the lack of firm evidence in many of the cases. Additionally, there were significant problems with the legality of witness statements because of the inappropriate procedures used by the IG investigators. But by early May, Adm. Reason had eventually received case briefings on more than one hundred officers and judged not to pursue nearly half the cases. The remaining officers would be summoned to his Norfolk office to be adjudicated.

Over the next two months, the vast number of aviators chose the "admiral's mast" option and appeared with an attorney or other representative before Adm. Reason and argued their cases. Most of these officers had been charged with indecent exposure or "conduct unbecoming." Fines were levied; nonpunitive letters and letters of censure were given; and two cases were dismissed. However, a handful had opted out of admiral's mast and instead had chosen court-martial.

Lt. Gen. Chuck Krulak's official title was commander of the Marine Corps Combat Development Command located about fifty miles south of DC on I-95 in Quantico, VA. After learning of his selection as CDA for those Marine Corps officers involved in Tailhook, like his Navy counterpart, he chose JAG officers who would oversee and be integral parts of the judicial process. His selected staff was not as large as Adm. Reason's since the number of Marine Corps cases was far fewer—only twenty-two. There was another significant difference, however. One of his cases involved victim number 50—Lt. Paula Coughlin.

After Krulak's staff had reviewed the files, three cases were dismissed and hearings on the remaining nineteen Marine Corps aviators began in late June. Similar to the Navy files, most cases involved minor offenses which were expected to be handled at "office hours"—the Marine Corps version of admiral's mast. Although there were obstacles, problems, and setbacks, by mid-August, all the minor cases had been addressed.

Then on August 17, "THE" important major pretrial hearing began.[44] The accused was Marine Corps Capt. Gregory Bonam, an African-American, F/A-18 pilot who was now serving as a jet training instructor in Meridian, Mississippi. Lt. Coughlin was the first prosecution witness in the Article 32 hearing which is similar to a grand jury proceeding. It was being conducted in a Quantico courtroom by Colonel Steven Mitchell, a Marine Corps Reserve judge. After the prosecution's witnesses were completed, Capt. Bonam testified in his own defense denying he was the man whom Coughlin had identified as one of her gauntlet attackers. Several other officers testified on his behalf. The hearing was adjourned later that same day but reopened nearly two months later after Bonam's defense attorney discovered a key eye witness to Coughlin's assault.

James Kelly was a Navy civilian employed at NAS Patuxent River where Lt. Coughlin had been based as aide to Adm. Snyder. He personally knew her and had also attended Tailhook. He testified that he witnessed the gauntlet on Saturday night and had seen Coughlin being manhandled. He testified that Capt. Bonam wasn't the man who grabbed and held Coughlin. He described the assailant as a man with significantly different physical characteristics than those of Bonam. Several other witnesses corroborated details which Bonam had testified to which clearly undercut Coughlin's testimony that Bonam was her assailant. At the end of the hearing, Bonam's attorney asked that all charges be dropped.

A week later, on October 21, Gen. Krulak dismissed the case saying, through a spokesman, that the facts didn't support the charges.[45] There was relief and jubilation for Capt. Bonam and his supporters but disappointment and disbelief for Paula Coughlin, the officer who had first blown the whistle on Tailhook more than twenty-four months before.

The author on the fantail of Walter Cronkite's *WYNJTE.* (1993)

Stefanie (then girlfriend) and author at NAS North Island to attend Capt. Jim Maslowski's Change-of-Command of the USS *Kitty Hawk* (CVA-63). (1992)

Adm. Jay Miller (at the lectern), Adm. Jack Moriarty and the author at his retirement ceremony. (1994)

The “912 Gang”. L-r: Tim Martin, Bob McMurray, Luke Colbert, Bill Brown, Fred Celce, Mike Ashford, Pete Nevins, author. (1985)

Capt. Mike Ashford relaxing aboard *WYNJTE.* (1993)

Walter Cronkite checking a nav map aboard *WYNJTE*
while Capt. Jeff and Mike Ashford look on. (1993)

Walter Cronkite relaxing aboard his *WYNJTE.* (1993)

Secretary John Lehman cruising aboard *WYNJTE.* (1993)

Friends aboard the USS *John F. Kennedy* (CV-67), July 4, 1986, to celebrate the relighting of the STATUTE OF LIBERTY. (1986)

Three "Hell's Sissies" at "Rolling Thunder", Washington, D.C. L-r: Pete Nevins, author, John Ashmore. (1988)

The New York Athletic Club Water Polo Team. The author is front row, fourth from the left. His buddy, Jack Atkinson, is third from left. (1962)

Former SECNAV John H. Dalton and the author at the Navy-Duke football game. (2013)

Cruising with the "Boys"

"Sensational."

THE SUMMER HAD FLOWN BY with too much time and effort spent agonizing over Tailhook. Fortunately, I had an event that was fast approaching which, I hoped, would set my mind right. In early September, Mike, my pal, called me and asked if I'd like to sign up as a crew member for *a Wynjte* cruise from either Martha's Vineyard or New York City to Annapolis in the beginning of October. Beginning in the late '70s, I had received similar invitations from Mike and always participated if I could adjust my Navy and airline schedules. Mike had been assigned this crew scheduling job which he performed brilliantly.

The current *Wynjte* was a forty-eight-foot ketch-rigged yacht, custom built in 1986 in Wilmington, North Carolina, by Sunward Yachts for its owners, Walter and Betsy Cronkite. In fact, my 912 biplane partner, Fred, and I were on its maiden voyage in the Cape Fear River in 1986 with the Cronkites and their children, Nancy, Kathy, and Chip and some other friends including Andy Rooney and Bill Harbach. When Mike told me the names of the other prospective crew members he was recruiting, I didn't even think about the difficulties associated with getting the necessary days off. I just said, "Hell yes, sign me up!" In addition to Walter and his captain, Jeff, all but one of the crew had sailed with me multiple times before: Mike, Fred, and John Lehman. The only "new guy" was a longtime friend, ex-air force and Delta pilot, Jim Welldon.

These cruises had begun in the late '70s after Walter and Betsy had attended an Annapolis event during a stopover while sailing their previous forty-two-foot Westsail *Wynjte* from their Edgartown home on the Vineyard to Florida via the Intracoastal Waterway. Mike and Carol, his wife, had hosted the affair at their Severn River home and invited Walter and Betsy to join them afterward for dinner at McGarvey's. While entertaining them there, Mike introduced Luke, Fred, and me to them, and we all partied until late into the evening. Thus began an extraordinary friendship between Walter and Mike which fortunately included us sharing in many wonderfully exciting times with the "Commodore" at the helm.

In addition to being a crew member on the sail down to or back from Florida or the Caribbean, I had been their sailing guest/ crew member several times in the British Virgin and other Leeward Islands and waters around the Vineyard and the Maine coast. No matter where or when, the experience of being part of a Cronkite entourage always turned into a memorable event. After I hung up, I was already looking forward to having another sail filled with good times with the "boys."

I managed to rearrange my October schedule such that after I returned to Washington National Airport, on my two-day trip, I immediately flew up to LaGuardia with my sailing gear. I arrived at Stefanie's Upper East Side apartment around 7:00 PM where I changed clothes out of my uniform into civies and went to one of Stef's favorite local restaurants, Campagnola, which featured her favorite dinner, Osso Bucco. We had a wonderful time with another couple who were two of her longtime New York friends. As I had an early departure time, we called it a night way before Stef had wanted.

Wednesday morning we were out of her building by 7:00 AM, my sailing gear in tow as we walked the several blocks to the subway which we rode to the Fulton Street Station. As we approached the South Street Seaport, I easily recognized *Wynjte* docked there. A couple of minutes later, we were on deck exchanging greetings with Walter, Mike, Fred, and Jimbo. Jeff was busy bringing some last-minute provisions aboard. As this was the first time Stef had met Walter, she was excited and enthused. Ever the gentleman and humorist, Walter hinted that "maybe we should leave Bobby here and take *Stefanie* with us to Annapolis." All of us chuckled at that suggestion, which I half thought was sincere!

A few minutes later, John Lehman came walking out on the pier carrying his sea bag and joined everyone on deck. As he and I were the last to arrive, all the berthing spaces had already been claimed except the very forward and less desirable v-berths. John suggested that we "flip" to decide who picks first but I thought we should do it by naval "seniority." I reminded him that if we were doing this when he had been SECNAV, he would have made the first pick. However, given that my date of rank as a Navy Reserve captain was before his, the choice was mine. As I had studied the forecast weather and winds beforehand and determined that we'd have a stiff easterly wind during the first leg from New York Harbor to the entrance to the Delaware Bay, I chose the starboard berth—John just chuckled and threw his bag on the port v-berth.

We said our good-bye's to our loved ones, took in all the lines, and got underway. The sailing conditions were ideal—blue skies, fifteen knots of wind, and away we sailed. We were making about 7.5 kts as we cruised under the Verrazano Narrows Bridge and later made our turn to the southwest after passing Sandy Hook, New Jersey. We sailed parallel to and ten to twenty miles off the New Jersey coastline. As the seas were relatively calm, the sail was relaxing and the mood carefree.

We were set up as three two-man, four-hour watch teams. When not "on watch" at the helm, we either gathered in groups in the cockpit or in the main dining area or separately found a suitable place to read a book or have chats with one another. One of the highlights was dining together—especially dinner—as that was when Walter would entertain us with his many interesting stories. I always felt disappointed when the after-dinner get-togethers broke up. There were always more incredible stories to hear but never enough time for Walter to tell them.

More often than not, the tales told had to do with our military experiences. Walter, of course, could talk about his WWII, Korea, and Vietnam stories as a combat reporter. Mike, Jimbo, and Fred were all Air Force jet pilots. Mike had flown the eight-engine B-47 Bongo bomber while Fred and Jimbo had flown the "Hun," the F-100 Super Sabre fighter. John had first been a naval flight officer and had flown, as a bombardier/navigator, the A-6 Intruder during Reserve active-duty periods from carriers in Vietnam. While on Henry Kissinger's White House staff, he had also flown close air support missions in the OV-10 Bronco in South Vietnam. Years later, he qualified for and received his Naval Aviators Wings in 1981. As the youngster of the group, I could call upon my experiences flying the A-7 on combat missions in Vietnam and the RF-8 Photo Crusader in the '70s and '80s.

I was not disappointed after our first at-sea dinner ended. Initially, the mood and talk were rather subdued but conversations became more lively midway through. By the time we were having coffee and desert, the banter was fast-paced and animated. Good-natured jabs were given and received especially when interservice rivalry was the topic. Witnessing the spectacle, I was reminded of the scenes of the officers' mess aboard Capt. Jack Aubrey's beloved *Sophie*.

That first evening we had a pleasant run down south. We rounded Cape May, New Jersey, and entered the channel entrance to the Delaware Bay at 3:00 AM. John and I had the midnight to 4:00 AM "dog" watch but from 2:00 AM, Jeff was also in the cockpit with us. Anticipating more than a ninety-degree heading change, Walter had thought Jeff might be needed to ensure that all sail changes were made safely and efficiently. As it turned out, we experienced a significant wind shift which resulted in a simple tack to enter and stay in the channel. John and I were relieved by 3:45 AM and hit our racks shortly thereafter.

Around 8:00 AM, I awoke to the smell of bacon and coffee. A quick outdoor shower, change of clothes, and I joined the rest of the crew for breakfast. Everyone was in a happy mood as the weather conditions continued to be perfect. We were now doing about 7 kts as we sailed up thru the Delaware Bay "wing and wing." We took in the sails and started the engine several hundred yards before we made the westerly turn to enter the Chesapeake and Delaware Canal. Sometime later, Walter, Mike, Fred, and I were together on deck as we motored past Schaefer's Restaurant in Chesapeake City. This was one of Walter's favorite places where we frequently had dinner and spent the night. Since on this journey, we had several more hours available to sail before nightfall, Walter opted to press on.

By 5:00 PM, we reached the entrance to the Sassafras River, which is an eastern tributary of the Chesapeake Bay on the Delmarva Peninsula. Our destination was Back Creek, an anchoring area about eight miles east. At 6:30 PM, we successfully "set the hook" and prepared for happy hour. Some of us went for a refreshing swim before we showered and changed into dinner dress. What soon followed was the essence of why we so thoroughly enjoyed these sails: to quote Mike, it was "whopping it up with the boys." For the next four hours, we enjoyed the company of each other sharing in the comrade-in-arms brotherhood which is distinct from any other group I've ever been a part of. After the brandy sniffers were emptied and the cigars extinguished, Walter aptly described the evening's festivities with but one word: "Sensational."

The loud clattering sound of the anchor chain raising the hook startled me out of my deep sleep. By the time I got a cup of coffee and went topside a few minutes later, we were motoring out of our overnight hideaway. This morning, the 10-kt wind had shifted further to the north, so we waited until we reached the channel in the bay before we deployed the sails. Once set, the ride was as comfortable as it gets.

As all sailors who have ever done the Intracoastal Waterway in the bay, the eastern ship channel is extremely narrow in many areas. Careful adherence to navigational maps and the marked buoys is mandatory. By early afternoon, we were in a very narrow channel which hugged the Eastern Shore coastline. The newest member of our group, Jimbo, had the con and was at the ship's helm. He had been instructed as to what heading to steer by the Commodore himself. Most of us were engaged in other activities and not really paying much attention to navigation when suddenly the boat seemed to take a lurch forward and then almost came to a stop. Jeff, who was sitting directly behind Jimbo, instantly knew what had happened and instructed Jimbo to "turn starboard thirty degrees." Due to the direction and force of the tides, *Wynjte* had been pushed out of the channel and had brushed her keel along the sandy bottom of the bay. Quickly we were back in the channel as if nothing happened except that Jimbo was mortified. Some of us consoled him as best we could telling him that he was now inaugurated properly, as at one time or another each of us was at the helm when we "almost" went aground. I knew that he would eventually get over it because all of us did—it was just a matter of time and circumstance.

We soon sailed under the Chesapeake Bay Bridge and made the turn north up the Severn River. We passed by the Naval Academy and tied up at Mike's dock at the Stately Ashford Manor, a few hundred yards south of the Route 50 Bridge. The obligatory postsail drinks were served for an hour or so before we prepared for dinner at McGarvey's. I went home, unpacked, showered, and shaved and headed to the saloon.

Friday nights are always crowded at Mike's establishment, but this one was exceptionally so. By the time I arrived, the entire crew had already been served and was in animated conversations in the front bar. Of course, "Uncle Walter" was surrounded by many Annapolitan admirers. Occasionally, I glanced over his way and would see him, Mike, and John totally immersed in lively discourses. Eventually, Jimmy, Mike's manager, let all of us know that the Aviator Room was set for us and soon we were all seated. This "end of the cruise" dinner was another fantastic event which lasted well past midnight. As I had to fly my trip the next morning, it was time for me to head home. I said my good-byes to everyone and thanked Walter and Mike for including me as a crew member. Not just another memorable cruise, this one had been extraordinary!

Tailhook '91

"I'd be delighted to keep him company."

PART OF MY "ALONE TIME" aboard *Wynjte* had been spent reading and thinking about all the incredibly detailed incidents in "Part 2" of the IG report. This had prompted me to review my recollection of the events at the Hilton Hotel which I had witnessed two years before. Part of this exercise was my attempt to recall the points which I made in my Tailhook debrief report. I had provided the two-page document to Adm. Dunleavy a few days after I returned home from Las Vegas. Unfortunately, I had not kept a copy.

Now back from the cruise to retrace my steps, I first consulted my airline schedule for the month of September '91. I was at that time, a first officer on the B-737, based in Washington, DC. Because I was a relatively junior copilot, that meant that I would not get a good monthly flight schedule since those were awarded to more senior United pilots. It didn't look good for me attending Tailhook since the September flight schedule I received in mid-August had me flying a three-day trip over the Friday, Saturday, and Sunday, September 6–8, which were the symposium days. I immediately started to try to trade my trips with other copilots to free up those days. Despite my best efforts, I was unsuccessful. By Thursday, September 5, which was the first official Tailhook day, I had just about given up. But my phone rang around 6:00 pm, and it was a first officer friend who desperately needed to trade his identical three-day trip which departed late afternoon on Sunday. If I would take his trip on Sunday, then he would take mine on Friday. I immediately signed up, and we coordinated the exchange with the United crew scheduling office.

The next step was to figure out how to get out to Vegas. A few phone calls later, I discovered that there was a nonstop USAir flight from Baltimore-Washington International (BWI) to Vegas which left early the next morning and would get me out there shortly before noon. At the same time, I checked into the return trip and was fortunate to find a USAir flight from Vegas back to BWI leaving at 11:30 pm, Saturday Evening and arriving back at BWI at 7:00 am on Sunday morning. The next obstacle was where to stay.

I had previously chatted with Tailhook Association people and learned that there were no rooms available at the Hilton, so I found out the name of the hotel where United pilots stay during Vegas layovers. I called the Holiday Inn and arranged a room for just Friday night since I'd be taking the all-nighter back on Saturday in order to make my scheduled UAL flight on Sunday evening. I then called my ex-roomie Jack Moriarty in Jacksonville, FL, and left a message explaining to him that I had just completed all the arrangements for getting to Vegas and I'd see him there at some point.

Everything was falling happily into place!

The next morning, I got to the USAir gate and spoke with the gate agent who signed me up for the jump seat. Once aboard, the captain and head flight attendant offered an empty coach seat to me, which I gladly accepted. As there was an empty middle seat, the five-hour ride was comfortable and relaxing. We arrived early, and I took a courtesy van directly to the Hilton where I checked my luggage and headed for the Tailhook Association check-in desk. After registering and signing up for Saturday night's dinner, I headed straight to the pavilion area.

While I had missed several important events earlier in the morning, including the symposium introduction by Adm. Dunleavy and Capt. Ludwig, I managed to hear and see four senior naval aviators discuss Desert Storm Naval Operations. Capt. "Ho Chi" Bien was the senior naval aviator on the JFACC (Joint Forces Air Component Command) in Riyadh, Saudi Arabia. JFACC, commanded by USAF Lt. Gen. Chuck Homer, was responsible to the JFC (Joint Force Commander), US Army Gen. Normal Schwarzkopf, for "coordinating, planning, deconflicting, and executing the overall air campaign to meet the JFC's guidance and objectives." Listening to his presentation made me more aware of the difficult position Naval Air was in when operating as only a minor participant in an organization that was predominantly run by the Air Force.

His presentation was followed by Capt. Burin who was CAG 5 (commander, Carrier Air Wing) aboard USS *Midway (CVA-43)* operating in the Persian Gulf. His presentations resulted in an appreciation of how complex and demanding those strike sorties had been. Next up was Capt. "Fox" Fallon who was CAG-8 aboard USS *Theodore Roosevelt (CVN-71)*. He, too, described, in detail, many aspects of the battle: the threats, the weapons employed, long-range ops, weather-related issues, coordination problems, etc. Finally, Marine Corps Col. Beaufant described what the war was like from the prospective of the Corps. After his brief, I was glad to know that the Marine Corps was able to do a remarkable job despite all the obstacles—many dealing with "jointness" issues.

After a short lunch break, I attended the "Tomahawk" (cruise missile) and air-to-ground weapons programs. As I was a former light-attack pilot, both subjects interested me, and I came away impressed at how far we've come since my years of dropping "dumb" bombs in Vietnam. At this point, I decided not to attend the air-to-air brief but instead retrieved my baggage and took a short cab ride to Holiday Inn where I checked in, showered, and changed clothes. I returned to the Hilton just in time to attend the briefing on TARPS (Tactical Air Reconnaissance Pod System). This was the replacement for the internal cameras carried in the RF-8 Photo Crusader, which was the last purely photo reconnaissance naval aircraft which had been retired in 1986. The TARPS "pod" was a canoe-shaped structure containing multiple cameras and was attached to the underbelly of an F-14 Photo Tomcat. I was interested in hearing their talk as I remember back in the early '80s when TARPS was first introduced to Fighter Squadrons. That new role was as welcome to that community "as a case of VD," or so they told us. Although it appeared as though they begrudgingly had accepted the photo mission, they continue to think of themselves primarily as "fighter jocks."

The next two events I attended had much larger crowds: MIG killers and POWs. A Navy lieutenant and Marine Corps captain described their MIG 29 shoot downs. It turned out that during the Q&A session which followed, one of the comments came from a well-known Soviet pilot who had defected to Turkey in a MIG-29 in the late '80s. The audience went wild.

The firsthand POW brief was given by three aviators who were POWs for two or three months. You could have heard a pin drop as we listened to their personal experiences which were riveting. This was followed by a brief on the strike rescue operations and how they were coordinated and executed by the joint forces. As I was pretty much up-to-date about the F-18 E/F and future strike fighter plans, I decided to forego these briefs and instead go out to the pool/patio area to see if I could find my buddy Jack Moriarty.

As the weather was beautiful but the temperature hot and the pool looked so good, I wished I had brought along a swimsuit. I grabbed a beer from one of the hospitality suites, found a comfortable lounge chair, and just relaxed. I must have dozed off for a while because when I grabbed my once cold beer can it was now lukewarm. I got up and walked around looking for Jack but instead met several old friends from my Navy and airline careers. I happened to locate a house phone and left a message on Jack's room answering service that I would remain by the pool area until 8:30 pm or so, and then I'd be returning to my hotel room and retiring after I got something to eat. If I didn't meet up with him tonight, I'd try him tomorrow morning—but not early.

By this time, there was no denying that the size and noise level of the poolside crowd had increased significantly. I walked over to another suite and grabbed a cold one and went back to the patio. As I was standing there, I saw three familiar faces, Admirals Dunleavy, Kelso, and Fetterman, and they were headed my way. I greeted all three, and we exchanged pleasantries. My former Boss told me that he and his buddy Jack Fetterman had some places to visit and asked if I'd mind keeping the CNO occupied until they returned. "I'd be delighted to keep him company," I said, and off they went back in the direction of the suites. The CNO and I engaged in small talk as we drank our beverages. He asked where I was stationed, and I told him I was a Reserve captain who had been working for Adm. Dunleavy in OP-O5 as the Reserve unit's CO. Prior to that, I told him that I had worked as the Navy Department duty captain in the Navy Command Center where I had seen him quite regularly. At that point, there was some commotion and loud chanting from a nearby crowd which we both saw and heard. We exchanged some commentary about what was happening, but the incident quickly came to an end. After that, the CNO said he was going to look around, so we said our good-byes.

Rather than search for a place for dinner, I decided to get something to eat at the Hilton whose buffet dinner suited me to a tee. After a delightful dinner at a table I shared with a couple of SNAs (student naval aviators) from Kingsville, I walked back to my hotel room. A short while later, I called it a night.

In the morning, after an early getup, I took advantage of a well-equipped workout room and indoor swimming pool for an hour and a half. I packed up my bag and got to the Hilton about 8:30 am. I called Jack's room, and he was there having just returned from participating in the Tailhook 5K run which had begun at 7:00 am. I brought my luggage up to his room and left it there. We then had breakfast and discussed what we thought of the symposium so far. While Jack needed to attend the morning sessions due to his professional obligations, I opted to visit the many vendor exhibits in the massive hall. Exploring and learning what all the Navy and Defense Department contractors were trying to sell was the main purpose but not the only one. Collecting all sorts of goodies that most vendors gave away was an integral part of the Tailhook experience. T-shirts, mugs, sunglasses, playing cards, and posters were just a few of the collectable items I picked up. While I was doing this, Jack attended the awards luncheon and heard Dunleavy's "State of Naval Aviation" address, which I had previously read bits and pieces of during my workdays at the OP-05 offices.

At 2:20 pm, as we had planned, Jack and I met and found two seats in the almost filled auditorium to witness the Flag Panel, which is the major event of the symposium. The onstage panel included all the "heavies" of Naval Aviation. This year, it consisted of six three-stars (five Navy and one Marine Corps) and three two-stars (Navy). I had previously worked for, or knew personally, all but Lt. Gen. Wells (HQMC) and Rear Adm. J. L. Johnson (BUPERS) and the moderator Capt. Fred Ludwig. For almost four hours, the panel essentially had an open discussion with mostly JOs about every aspect of their professional lives. The question which was the most highly anticipated, "When will women fly and fight in combat?" was eventually asked by a female aviator. It was answered by Dunleavy whose "bull's-eye" shirt was most appropriate considering the pointed and sometimes harsh criticism he had been subjected to. After the loud moans and groans of the audience had dissipated, the Boss said that if and when the legislation which authorized it were passed, the Navy would implement it as directed. A JO sitting near me sprung up from his chair and suggested to the admiral that was not the answer he expected since he knew that, in effect, this was a male-only role. After the subsequent cheers of approval had subsided, Dunleavy essentially repeated his previous message using slightly different words.

After the panel ended, Jack and I went to his room where we changed into coats and ties and proceeded to the no-host cocktail party for a short time and then to the Saturday-night concluding banquet. We recognized many friends and had short conversations with a few. Both Adm. Kelso and SECNAV Garrett were in attendance, and Garrett was the featured speaker. He spoke of the great performance of Carrier Aviation during the war but also addressed the many serious challenges facing the community. In the end, like in so many past times, he said he was confident that Naval Aviation would overcome all the obstacles and prosper.

I tried to make the most of the few minutes before I had to leave. I had brief conversations with Admirals Dunleavy, Fetterman, Kohn, and Less, and then Jack and I hustled back to his room where

I did a quick change into my travelling clothes. Jack accompanied me to the lobby where we said our good-byes right before I jumped into a cab which took me to the airport.

Once again at the departure gate, I signed up for the USAir jump seat. After I boarded and introduced myself to the captain, I was offered a first-class seat back to BWI. Just before I dozed off, I was thinking how lucky I had been to be at this incredible event. What a fantastic success this symposium had been—it could not have been better!

Courts-Martial Proceedings

"Am I hearing what I think I'm hearing?"

SOON AFTER NOMINATION TO BE the secretary of the Navy on July 1, 1993, John Dalton necessarily became intimately involved with the Tailhook investigations. I had first met my new Navy boss under less than friendly terms in September 1962 at the Naval Academy. Along with 1,200 other young men, I had successfully made it through the rigors of "plebe summer," but now, after all the upperclassmen had returned from their summer cruises, the entire 4,200-man "Brigade of Midshipmen" was in residence. The daily lives of we plebes had dramatically changed because during the summer, there were only about 150 second-classmen (juniors), members of the class of 1964, stationed at the Academy to train the incoming class of 1966. The ratio of upper class to plebes had been 1:10; now it was 3:1, which meant far more attention would be paid to the "professional development" of each plebe by upperclassmen—primarily second-classmen (juniors).

"Big John," as he was then known, was a well-liked and respected member of the second class, who took seriously performing his role of "running the plebes"—a more politically acceptable term than *hazing*. "Running" encompassed all aspects of the indoctrination, discipline, and professional growth of a plebe.

Mental, psychological, and physical pressures (many now would call them "abuses") were liberally used to test the mettle and dedication of each member of the class of '66. In his role as mentor, I remember him to have been stern but fair.

During the next two years, along with his friend and classmate, Ted Gordon, the three of us remained as Seventeenth Company comrades living close by one another in Bancroft Hall and occasionally eating our meals at the same ten-man mess hall table. We rarely had any other personal contact since Dalton and I were in two different year groups and shared no common interests in extracurricular or sports activities. In his senior year, he was a "high striper" within the midshipmen organization, meaning he was awarded high-ranking positions of leadership within the brigade by the commissioned officers who comprised the administration of the Academy. He had, as we used to say, "grease," Navy slang for influence or aptitude for naval service.

After being sworn in as the Navy's sixty-seventh secretary on July 22, 1993, he now had to use that grease and all the other his skills he had acquired to effectively navigate through a political mine field. I could not help but wonder if he had read a fellow ring knocker's *Washington Post* editorial written months before.[46] Retired Adm. Stansfield Turner had warned that the incoming secretary of the Navy was going to inherit a can of "Tailhook worms." The case he made might well have scared off lesser individuals—but not Big John, I guessed.

Still unresolved was a section of the DoD IG report which contained files about the thirty-five flag officers (thirty-three Navy and two Marine) who had attended Tailhook '91. Upon studying those files, Dalton no doubt realized that he needed to address this most serious and contentious issue. Since the report involved the CNO himself and many of his high-ranking colleagues, it was a political "hot potato" whose players held the highest offices at the White House and Pentagon.

After months of examination which included his own "personal interviews" with each of the flags, the secretary announced on October 15 that he was giving three admirals Secretarial Letters of Censure: Vice Adm. Richard Dunleavy and Rear Admirals Riley Mixson and Wilson Flagg.[47] Additionally, he was permanently reducing Dunleavy's rank to rear admiral. He gave thirty admirals and generals less severe Nonpunitive Letters of Caution. Two admirals who were not in attendance on Saturday night were absolved.

His blockbuster announcement sent shock waves throughout the Naval Aviation community. The immediate response from the most junior flyer to the most senior was anger and disbelief. Everyone realized that most, if not all, of the thirty-three flags just had their careers effectively ended.

For Adm. Dunleavy who had been retired almost sixteen months, the Letter of Censure, though harsh, was not unexpected by many of us. In fact, for months in early 1991, he had made it clear to everyone that he fully accepted responsibility for the debacle and was quoted in a May 6, 1992, *Los Angeles Times* interview that "I should be fired." On the other hand, making his reduction from three-star to two-star status permanent in retirement was seen as grossly unfair. Moreover, Dalton's extracting his pound of flesh at this point was seen by many as being purely vindictive in nature.

For Mixson, it took only hours before he issued a response to SECNAV Dalton's letter. From his OP-05 Pentagon office, he issued his first rebuttal, in which he denied any misconduct but said, "If, by this action, we have finally come one step closer to closing the book on this regrettable chapter of Naval Aviation, then I am truly gratified." But just three days later, he made public his formal four-page rebuttal which took the secretary to task for multiple and significant factual inaccuracies in his assertions and conclusions. "In your heart, you know that I am being made a scapegoat for the lack of proactive leadership of those in direct operational and administrative chain of command, those in charge of those who committed misconduct... Two wars, years at sea, absolute loyalty and dedication to my Navy and my country, and you are punishing me as if I were guilty of misconduct."[48]

Eight days later, Rear Adm. Flagg delivered his two-page rebuttal, which first challenged Dalton's assertion that he had witnessed inappropriate behavior during his attendance.[49] He denied both seeing or taking part in any misconduct.

He reiterated again to the secretary that he had departed the symposium on Friday night, so he could not have witnessed the misconduct on Saturday night. In his prepared announcement, Sec. Dalton had made it clear that he had singled out Dunleavy, Mixson, and Flagg because they alone "played key roles in the organization and administration of Tailhook '91." The problem was, however, that neither Mixson nor Flagg was actually involved. Mixson hadn't arrived in OP-05 until June 1991 and Flagg was not there at all—he was stationed in Norfolk at the offices of Commander, Naval Air Atlantic (AIRLANT). The other serious inaccuracy with Dalton's position was that the Tailhook Association, not OP-05, was responsible for the vast majority of the organization-related functions and activities. Perhaps, the real reason why SECNAV had chosen these three for the severest punishments was best summed up by Mixson who commented that they "bear the brunt of what you perceive as a 'politically correct decision.'"

Like so many others in Naval Aviation, I was personally affected by the cases of Admirals Mixson and Flagg, both of whom I had known for a long time. Adm. Mixson had been a fellow A-7 Corsair pilot based in Lemoore back in the Vietnam era. In 1970–1971, he had been a member of VA-195, the "Dambusters," based aboard the USS *Kitty Hawk (CVA-63)* in the Tonkin Gulf—the same time period when I was there on the *Ranger* with VA-113. His squadron had a colorful and honored history. During the Korean War flying the venerable A-1D "Spad," the squadron had successfully bombed and destroyed a North Korean dam and so adopted their moniker. He later commanded the "Barn Owls" of VA-215, another A-7 squadron and then later CVWR-30, the other Reserve Carrier Air Wing of which our sister Reserve squadron at Andrews, VFP-306, was part. He had also had been the CO of the carrier USS *Midway (CVA-41).*

Most significantly, prior to reporting to OP-05 as Adm. Dunleavy's deputy in June 1991, he had commanded Battle Force

Yankee, also known as the Red Sea Battle Group during the Gulf War's Operation Desert Shield and later Desert Storm. Yankee was composed of two carrier groups which included the USS *Saratoga* and USS *John F. Kennedy*. Both played a significant role in the execution of the First Gulf War.

I had first met then Cdr. Wilson "Bud" Flagg in 1977 when I was undergoing initial qualification training in the RF-8G Photo Crusader at Naval Air Facility Washington located at Andrews Air Force Base. After becoming certified, I was subsequently selected to join VFP-206, one of the two Reserve Navy photo squadrons based at Andrews. Bud was then its commanding officer, and for the next year, I worked for him as one of the pilots as well the squadron's landing signal officer.

He was a dynamic and colorful leader whose exemplary commanding officer performance was capped with our squadron winning a prestigious Naval Reserve award. On the personal side, Bud possessed a friendly and jovial personality and always had an amusing story or joke to tell. Bud was a legend among the close-knit F-8 community whose members flew the plane known both as the "MiG Master" and the "Last of the Gunfighters." He had amassed more than 3,700 hours in the venerable "Sader" far surpassing his closest rival. Like several of us in the squadron, Bud was a commercial airline pilot employed by American Airlines as a Boeing 727 captain. Coincidentally, from 1985 to 1987, as a Navy captain, he had previously worked for Adm. Dunleavy when the admiral was commander, Carrier Group Four based in Norfolk. As a mentor of mine, Bud had encouraged me to apply for the job as CO of OP-05 as he had a very high regard for Adm. Dunleavy. After I had subsequently been selected to be the CO of the Reserve OP-05 unit, Bud was one of the first to call and congratulate me. He wished me well and extended an invitation to get in touch with him if I ever needed his help or advice. Our paths crossed several times during my tour at OP-05 and no matter what, a meeting with Bud always left a big smile on my face.

While in Washington the Navy establishment was abuzz with the news of the flag officers' punishments, it wasn't the only Navy city dealing with Tailhook. After several months of pretrial motions and procedural maneuverings, the legal proceedings in a naval court house in Norfolk, Virginia, seemed to be finally coming to a conclusion in the courts-martial of Navy Commanders Thomas R. Miller and Gregory E. Tritt. For months, their defense teams had successfully argued multiple motions before Navy Judge Capt. William T. Vest eliminating all their criminal charges. What remained were lesser charges relating to their witnessing and then failing to take actions to stop "inappropriate behavior" of their subordinates.

Cdr. Miller's court-martial began on November 8. One of the first motions his attorneys, LCDR William Little and Don Marcari, filed was a motion to dismiss because "unlawful command influence had been exercised" since the CNO, Adm. Kelso, had observed the same "inappropriate behavior" as Miller. Further, they contended, that since the CNO had already received a letter of reprimand from Sec. Dalton, Adm. Kelso was therefore prevented from being an "accuser" as defined by the UCMJ.

The following week, Cdr. Tritt's attorneys, Robert Rae, Alan Bergstrom, and LCDR Diane Karr joined Miller's motion to dismiss Tritt's case, as well, for the same reasons relating to the CNO. Capt. Vest subsequently joined both cases and then ordered Admirals Kelso, Dunleavy, Spane, and Fetterman and ex-SECNAV Garrett and UnderSECNAV Howard to appear in his courtroom on Monday, November 29.

In Judge Vest's standing-room-only courthouse, Adm. Kelso was sworn in and began testifying in midmorning. The defense attorneys' main thrust of their questions was to place him on the third-floor pool patio area and in the hospitality suites on Friday and Saturday evening—therefore witnessing the same inappropriate behavior as their clients. Despite Rae and his team naming various other witnesses who testified that they saw the CNO at these times and locations, he steadfastly denied his being on the third floor on Saturday night.

While acknowledging that he had, indeed, been on the pool patio area on Friday evening, he saw none of the inappropriate behavior described in specifics by the defense teams. Further, he denied ever going in any suites.

The prosecution team asked him questions which sought to show that he wasn't on the patio on Saturday night and hadn't witnessed any bad behavior on Friday night. They cited various witnesses who had confirmed the CNO's whereabouts as he had described. The prosecutors argued that there were several members of his staff, as well as his civilian former bosses who had given statements which supported his position. After two hours of testimony, Adm. Kelso was dismissed and a recess was declared.

After convening following the lunch break, Vice Adm. Dunleavy took the stand and in answering questions from the defense attorneys contradicted the CNO's testimony in one significant area of concern. He told the court that he and his longtime friend, Adm. "Jack" Fetterman, had personally escorted the CNO through a number of third-floor hospitality suites and then out on to the patio and pool area on Friday evening. Asked about seeing the CNO on the third floor on Saturday night, Dunleavy said he was not with him after the formal dinner and didn't see him anywhere on the third floor afterward.

A few days after their testimony, I travelled to Norfolk on Friday, December 3, to perform my Reserve weekend drills at my new assignment at Naval Station Norfolk. Having completed my two-year tour of duty as CO of the Navy IG in September, I had received orders to join the Reserve unit that supported CINCLANTFLT (commander-in-chief, Atlantic Fleet). I had made the same drive in early October and November. My weekends were hectic since, as a new guy, there was a great deal to learn, and I was eager to quickly get up to speed. I was worn-out by Sunday at 5:00 PM when I got into my car and made the return trip back to Annapolis arriving around 9:00 PM completely exhausted.

Late Tuesday afternoon, I checked in for my six-day international trip to Europe at United Airlines Operations Department at Dulles Airport and was excited to learn that a close friend, Andy Anderson, would be the captain of our three-man flight deck crew. Andy was a fellow naval aviator who had been a pilot at UAL for more than twenty-five years. He lived in a beautiful house on the water on Maryland's Eastern Shore only a few air miles from the

Easton Airport where I hangared my biplane. Most times when I took to the air, at some point during the flight, I'd fly close by his dock to let him know that I was "in the area." If he heard or saw me, he'd jump in his car with his cooler and be waiting for me to return to my hangar.

We'd share a few beers and always a few laughs.

This would, therefore, be an enjoyable trip, and I'd have someone to hang with in Frankfurt, Chicago, and London. Our trip, in pilots' shorthand lingo, was known as a "W" sequence. Our first leg would be from Dulles to Frankfurt arriving at 9:00 AM on Wednesday. We'd layover for a day and then fly to Chicago on Thursday morning arriving around 4:00 PM. After twenty-four hours in the "Windy City," we'd fly to London arriving there on Saturday morning. The following morning we'd fly back to Dulles arriving at 3:00 PM. Lots of flight time and many time zone changes made it rather difficult for your body's internal clock to adjust. But having a good crew made it much less stressful and therefore more "relaxing."

Typically, during my two-hour in-flight scheduled rest period on each of the four legs, I'd attempt to catch up on all my paperwork and reading materials which I had brought along. While comfortably seated in a back row seat in the first class section on Thursday's flight to Chicago on our Boeing 767-300, I began to read the December 1 issue of *Soundings*, a newspaper publication of the Military Newspapers of Virginia. I had picked this copy up during my weekend drills in Norfolk a few days before. One of the headline stories on the front page immediately got my attention: "Kelso, Garrett, Dunleavy take stand in Tailhook."[50] It was written by Jim Starling.

I first scanned the two-page article and then read and reread it underlining various quotes and passages. I then thought long and hard about what I had just read. My rest period ended and I returned to my copilot's seat in the cockpit. As I was relieving my friend Andy who would now go on break, I gave him the *Soundings* and asked him to read the Tailhook article. At the completion of his break, all three of us were now back in the cockpit, and we were only about an hour out from landing at O'Hare. Things necessarily were getting busy, so we agreed to talk about the article over beverages after we got to our layover hotel.

Several hours later, Andy and I were having drinks at a neighborhood "watering hole" while we waited to be seated for dinner. Andy was familiar with my Navy career as an aviator as we had previously traded fairly detailed life stories, so it didn't take very long to bring him up-to-date regarding my recent part in the ongoing Tailhook saga. Andy was a wonderful sounding board during the entire evening's discussion, providing thoughtful and well-considered insights into my dilemma.

After a restful sleep followed by a good workout and breakfast, I returned to my room where I used information to get the phone number of Cdr. Tritt's attorney, Robert Rae, in Norfolk. I called his office and eventually got him on the line. I informed him that I was a Navy captain and naval aviator who had followed the various Tailhook investigations and that I had just read the December 1 *Soundings* article which quoted the CNO's testimony. I told him that I had attended Tailhook '91 and that many of my former comrades were among the thirty-three flag officers who had recently received letters of reprimand from SECNAV. I then told him I would not be giving him my name—"not yet, at least." I asked him a question: "What effect would it have on the current cases, if someone testified that he was talking to the CNO, and while standing next to each other near the Hilton's third-floor pool, both witnessed something which now is considered to have been inappropriate behavior?" He responded that such testimony might be crucial to Tritt's and Miller's cases. I told him I needed to think about the consequences of testifying and that I'd get back to him on Sunday night. In the event I'd agree to testify, I told him I'd be able to get to Norfolk sometime Monday morning, as he had requested.

The flight to Heathrow Airport later that day, the layover in London and the return flight to Dulles were uneventful except for my growing angst. Andy and I had several conversations about the possibility of my upcoming court appearance which I now realized was something I was obligated to do. The only remaining question had to do with the logistics and mechanics of my upcoming travel plans.

The hour-long drive from employees' parking lot at Dulles to Annapolis on Sunday afternoon was relaxed and comfortable as there was little traffic on the Dulles access road, the capital beltway and Rt. 50. I was actually looking forward to reconnecting by phone with Robert Rae in a couple of hours. After arriving and unpacking, I changed into workout clothes and went for a bike ride around my favorite circuit: Quiet Waters and Bay Ridge. After cleaning up, I grabbed a beer and called the phone number Rae had previously given me.

This time after exchanging greetings, I introduced myself fully giving him a brief history of my naval career and the details of my Tailhook encounter with the CNO and Admirals Dunleavy and Fetterman. He asked several questions and seemed satisfied with all my responses. After I told him that I could travel the next day to Norfolk, he asked what time did I think I could meet with him. I had anticipated his question and had learned that I would be able to fly on a USAir jump seat pass on a 9:00 AM flight from BWI to Norfolk. I told him I'd probably be at his office on base by 11:00 AM if all went as planned. The twenty-minute call ended with me telling him that I was looking forward to meeting him and his associates and relating my story in the courtroom.

The next morning, my travel plans went as scheduled. Although I wore "civies" on the USAir plane, I changed into my Navy "blues" at the Norfolk airport. I took a cab to the office building on the naval base and got to the conference room shortly before 11:00 AM. In short order, I met Rae and Karr, Tritt's attorneys, and Little and Marcari, Miller's attorneys. Rae asked me to repeat to everyone the story which I had told him on Sunday. Several straightforward questions were posed about a few details of my time with the CNO. Additionally, one of them, Rae, I believe, asked me why I was coming forth and did I think that this might affect my possible promotion to admiral. I answered that I believed that I had an obligation to set the record straight and that I had considered the potential negative consequences of my testimony. Soon after that meeting, I met with the prosecuting attorneys to whom I repeated the same story. A few general questions were asked and then we took a short lunch break, during which I had a brief opportunity to socialize with the defense attorneys.

I found it most interesting to learn that Don Marcari was thought, at that time, to be the naval attorney who was portrayed in the movie *A Few Good Men* by Tom Cruise. (However, in 2011, Aaron Sorkin, its screenplay author, denied that it was based on "anyone.") The court went back into session, and soon after, I was called to appear. I walked in to a filled courtroom and was promptly sworn in. I scanned the room but saw no one I recognized. Rae asked questions to which I responded, essentially telling my Tailhook story which involved Adm. Kelso. I began by explaining to the court that I had been standing outside on the patio near the pool area early Friday evening having a beer by myself when I saw my former Boss, Adm. Dunleavy, along with Admirals Kelso and Fetterman. They came over to where I was standing and we exchanged greetings. Adm. Dunleavy asked me if I would be the CNO's escort for a while as he and Adm. Fetterman were going on a short tour. I told him that I'd be delighted, and they walked off heading toward the suites. After they departed, Adm. Kelso and I engaged in small talk as we consumed our beverages.

A few minutes elapsed, and then we heard a growing chant from a nearby group of young aviators. They were yelling, "Tits, tits, tits." I could see that the male crowd had surrounded a young woman in a bikini bathing suit. Adm. Kelso asked me, "Am I hearing what I think I'm hearing?" I answered, "Admiral, if you think you're hearing 'Tits,' you're absolutely right." It was obvious to me that they were trying to entice the girl to expose her breasts in exchange for a Tailhook T-shirt. It wasn't too long before a very loud cheer erupted as her top was thrown in the air. The CNO then said to me, "Well, I guess that's the end of that." I responded by saying, "Maybe, maybe not, Admiral." Within seconds, another chant started, this time it was, "Bush, bush, bush." It was clear that they wanted her to remove her bottoms. Now the size of the crowd was expanding, but hotel security arrived and broke up the group. The CNO at this point left my side and walked away. The total time of the event was less than a couple of minutes.

Mr. Rae asked me what prompted my appearance, and I told him about reading the CNO's quotes in the *Soundings* article about Admirals Dunleavy and Kelso's testimony. He also asked if I thought my appearance might affect my promotion to admiral. I answered by telling him I had considered that possibility.

After Ray's questions, the prosecutor asked me a few general questions one of which was, "Could you recognize the CNO?" I answered that I had seen the CNO many times while serving in various offices in the Pentagon over the previous several years. I added that he was easily identifiable.

I was dismissed, left the courtroom, and changed back into civies while I waited for a cab. I arrived at the airport in time to get on a 5:00 PM flight back to BWI. I took the employees' shuttle to the parking lot, quickly got into my car, and headed to Annapolis arriving around 8:00 PM. I headed straight to McGarvey's for drinks and dinner but mostly to debrief with several members of my gang whom I had previously asked to be there. In all probability, this was going to be a long night of conversations about my testimony and who better to ask the questions than my comrades.

Awaiting the Decision

"Well, Stanley, here's another fine mess you've gotten into."

When my bedside phone awakened me the next morning, my first reaction was absolute panic. "Aw shit, I'm screwed," I said out loud to myself thinking it must be United crew scheduling asking me why I hadn't checked in for my trip. In reaching for the phone, I noticed the time was 7:30 AM—much too early for that call and in the same instant realized that it was Tuesday and my next trip wasn't until Thursday.

I said, "Greetings, Bob Beck."

"Hey, Capt. Bob, it's your buddy, John, from Virginia Beach. How are you?"

"Holy crap, John, you scared the piss out of me. I had a very late outing with my friends in Annapolis last night and was sound asleep. I thought you were crew scheduling at United telling me I missed my scheduled flight. What's up with a seven-thirty wake-up call?"

He apologized for the early call but thought it important that I know something.

"I was just reading this morning's paper, and it had an article about your court appearance yesterday. I'm surprised you didn't tell me about this when we were drilling together two weeks ago."

"Two weeks ago, I had no idea that I'd be involved at all, but I had read something in a Norfolk paper last week about the ongoing trial and volunteered to testify just a few days ago. Any chance you could read it to me?" He told me he had to get to work but that he would fax it to me soon after he arrived at his office so I gave him my fax number. Before we signed off, I asked him what he thought of the article.

"Not long," he answered, "but very powerful."

I tried to gather my thoughts while I walked downstairs to the kitchen. I thanked my lucky stars that I had remembered to take three Excedrin before I fell into bed. Far too many times in the past after a late-night outing with Mike and the boys at McGarvey's, I had neglected to take any and the horrible result was a "MiG-15" hangover of epic proportions. MiGs were better known as "rusty nails" and were Mike's favorite nightcaps, and there was no way to turn them down. Fortunately, I "escaped" from his company when he went to the restroom, and I only drank two of them. I do admit, however, at the time they're served, it always seems like it's a great idea.

I watched TV while I waited for the coffee maker to do its thing. I thought it was funny that in all the conversations last night, no mention was made by anyone of media attention or reaction to my testimony. Now, however, because of my wake-up call, it had my undivided attention. I wondered how it was going to be received by people who knew me.

Around 9:00 AM, I heard the upstairs fax line ring and the machine "pick up." I refilled my coffee mug and carefully went up the spiral staircase to my fourth-floor office. I sat at my desk and started to read the one-page news clipping written by Kerry DeRochi, a *Virginian-Pilot* reporter: "Reservist: Kelso Heard Fliers Urge Woman to Strip."[51] It was one thing to testify in court and quite another to read my words on paper. In a word, it was "sobering." The article, I thought, was both accurate and fair in its description of my testimony. What disturbed me, however, was the reported reaction of Adm. Kelso to my testimony. In a Pentagon interview late Monday afternoon, he was quoted as saying, "I don't recall anything like that. I don't understand this. I don't have anything to hide."

After reflecting on his words, I realized that I shouldn't have expected anything different. The CNO's response to my account was exactly what his response had been in his courtroom testimony to all whose recollections differed from his. Essentially, he contended that he was right, and everyone who didn't agree with his version of the story was wrong. It seemed like it was a black-and-white issue with no gray area anywhere. All of a sudden, I realized I needed another Excedrin, but this time it had nothing to do with MIG-15s.

After my third cup of coffee, I decided that it was past time to get moving and exercise to clear the cobwebs and cleanse the system. Since the weather was dismal—rainy and cold—cycling and golf and all other outdoor activities were out of the question. I put on my Navy sweat gear over my swimsuit, jumped into my car, and headed over to the Academy's MacDonough Hall, which houses two Olympic-size swimming pools. I first went to the old practice pool, but it was being used by USNA class undergoing survival training. I then walked to another part of the enormous athletic facility to the Norman Scott Natatorium where, during my midshipman years, I had spent all my "spare" time as a member of the Navy swim team. It had since become the primary pool for water polo practice when the primary pool for the swim teams was relocated about a quarter mile away in the ultramodern Lejuene Hall sports complex constructed in 1982. I noticed that my friend, Water Polo Head Coach Mike Schofield, was in his office, so I paid him a short visit. He had come to the Academy in 1982 to help resurrect the varsity program after a thirty-two-year hiatus. In 1985, he took over as the head coach. Shortly after his arrival, I had introduced myself to him explaining that though I was on the Plebe and varsity swim teams, my first love had always been water polo, and I was so happy that it had regained varsity status at the Academy—it had been just an intramural "Battalion" sport during the gap, and I had played on my team all four years.

Mike had been the captain of the water polo team at Pittsburgh, graduating in 1979. During one of our early conversations, Mike had asked me how I was introduced to the sport, and I told him that as a freshman at Brooklyn Prep High School, a classmate buddy,

Jack Atkinson, who also swam on the BP team, had brought me along to the New York Athletic Club to play as a member of the Saturday Morning Boys' Club water polo team. In our junior year at high school, he and I had been asked by Charlie Schroeder, coach of the NYAC's men's team, to join his group and play on the Junior National Team. Since we were both fast swimmers and good ball handlers, we figured that we'd soon become first stringers. We had no idea the depth of talent and experience most of the men possessed, but we soon learned that in many cases, these men were national or international champions.

Many of our new teammates with whom we scrimmaged every Tuesday and Thursday evening from 7:00 to 9:00 PM were twice our age. Some had been on various Olympic teams—US and Hungarian. Some of the latter, in fact, had even been witness to one of the most famous events in Olympic history: The "Blood in the Water Match," which took place in the 1956 Summer Games in Melbourne, Australia, between Hungary and the USSR. The match was in the semifinal round which pitted the Hungarians, the reigning Olympic champs, against their overseers, the Russians. Two months before the December 6 match, Hungarian college students had begun a revolt seeking to have their homeland break away from the USSR. It seemed to be progressing well garnering widespread support from the US and the western European nations. Then in November, with little warning, the USSR employing the overwhelming power of its military, violently invaded the country and crushed the revolt.

Tensions were at the breaking point as the teams began the game. Although the Hungarians eventually won 4–0, it was a close game throughout and the action was fierce and violent with many fistfights breaking out during the game. The most famous scene and the one seared in my memory was a published photograph of Hungarian player, Ervin Zador, as he was being escorted from the pool with blood gushing from a head wound. Shortly thereafter, the game was halted before time officially ran out in order to avoid a riot by fans of both sides who had left their seats and gotten on to the pool deck. Hungary was declared the winner. They went on to win the Olympic title by defeating Yugoslavia 2–1 the next day. What then happened is legendary—more than half of the one-hundred-person Hungarian Olympic delegation defected, eventually relocating and playing water polo and other sports on teams in the US and Canada.

In the 1961 and 1962 seasons, of the thirty or so players who made up all the NYAC men's teams, there were about thirteen with whom I played on the Junior National Team, and of those, four were Hungarian players. Every one of them was a great guy, a remarkable player, and a friendly and fun-loving mentor. Jack and I were the two youngest players on the team and were fortunate to play in matches against other well-known athletic clubs, colleges, and universities from around the country. I always had a wonderful time travelling with these men to cities around the east coast and visiting different venues and campuses. By far, the most memorable event occurred during a tournament at the US Military Academy at West Point in May 1962—a mere two months before I began Plebe Summer at Annapolis.

We were participants in a three-day, Friday through Sunday, water polo tournament against mostly ivy league teams and a few other east coast colleges. As it happened, on Saturday afternoon on the parade field not too far from where the water polo matches were taking place, Gen. William Westmoreland, the forty-fifth superintendent of the Academy, presented the Sylvanus Thayer award to the thirty-first superintendent, five-star General of the Army, Douglas MacArthur. Later that afternoon, while standing high above the mess hall floor in a recessed balcony, the eighty-two-year-old general delivered what many historians believe to be one of the greatest speeches ever to have been given: his farewell address to the Corps of Cadets.

As all the water polo players were invited to eat their meals in the mess hall at the training tables, some of us witnessed this incredible performance. Anyone who has heard the recording of the speech or perhaps seen Gregory Peck deliver it in his portrayal of Gen. MacArthur in the movie *The American Caesar* can well imagine what an epic event it must have been to witness. It was truly a once-in-a-lifetime performance which left all who heard it essentially mesmerized.

During the concluding sentences, one could have heard a pin drop. When it ended, there seemed to be a prolonged silence, which was followed by the most thunderous applause I had ever heard, and it lasted a very long time. But it wasn't until many years later when I read William Manchester's book, upon which the movie is based, that I learned the background story of the speech. It is quite an extraordinary account that explains how the speech and accompanying theatrics were practiced and refined by a master performer.

I removed my sweats and dove into the pool and began my hour-long workout with a five-hundred-yard freestyle warm-up. Five two-hundred-yard moderately paced swims were next followed by five one-hundred-yard sprints and finally ten fifty-yard sprints. I had just finished my five-hundred-yard warm-down and was on the ladder getting out of the pool when I heard my name being called. It was Mike in the other end of the pool that was setup with water polo nets at both ends. I could see that he had several "mids" in the pool, and they were passing a water polo ball around. Mike asked me if I'd like to join in the practice session with members of his team.

Forty-five minutes later, while dragging myself out of the pool from the team scrimmage, I was reminded how exhausting this sport can be—especially to a body that in two weeks would be forty-nine years old. After showering, I changed into my street clothes and headed to McGarvey's for lunch. Even though it was still rainy and cold outside, the mood inside was welcoming and friendly. The doorman greeted me and told me that several of the boys were in the back room and that they had left word that I should join them if I showed up. As I was making my way through the front room, I said a quick hello to Capt. Mike who was making his rounds at the bar.

As I entered into the back room, I was pleased to see three of my friends, Luke, Fred, and Bob, who had been a part of last night's festivities. They were sitting at a table in the oyster bar section and had already been served their drinks. Being a firm believer in the "hair of the dog" adage, I promptly ordered what everyone else was drinking, a Bloody Mary, as I sat down. When the waitress asked for our orders a few minutes later, everyone chose the luncheon special, red beans and rice. This was a personal favorite of Mike who had instituted the tradition years before as a regular offering on Monday nights and Tuesday afternoons (if there were enough leftover.)

Small talk and funny stories ensued until our overflowing bowls of RBR were served, and then we all seriously dug in. Everyone agreed that this is exactly what our stomachs needed to fully recover. During a break in eating, I told everyone about my early-morning wake-up call in detail and then passed around the newspaper article.

The consensus was that there would definitely be negative consequences coming my way since all agreed that it had already become a question of whom to believe, and after all, Adm. Kelso was the chief of Naval Operations. I asked if anyone had read either today's *Washington Post* or *Baltimore Sun*, but no one had. It turned out that everyone had admitted to getting a very late morning start. Mike came over and sat down with us for a few minutes, during which time he read the article. Mimicking Oliver Hardy, he looked at me and in his best deadpan voice said, "Well, Stanley, here's another fine mess you've gotten into." Even I couldn't help but crack up laughing at Mike's inspired attempt at "gallows' humor."

As usual, the conversation soon turned to far lighter subjects and humorous personal stories, which always concluded with a good laugh. The topic which we focused on was tomorrow's motor cycle ride. Fortunately, the inclement weather that we were currently experiencing would be moving out to the northeast in the early evening and would be followed by a clear and cool late fall day—perfect conditions for a day trip into the country. So far, there would be eight bikes—seven Harleys and one Honda—meeting at Mike's house at 9:00 AM. We planned to ride ninety miles via the back roads to a restaurant near Calvert Cliffs, Maryland, where we'd have lunch. If all went well, we'd be back by late afternoon. Since it had been several months since our group, the "Hell's Sissies," took to the road, we were all looking forward to another great experience.

By the time I got back to my home from the saloon, it was early evening, and I was worn-out. I checked my answering machine and listened to several messages from friends and USNA classmates who had read various newspaper articles about my testimony in today's papers. My younger brother, Jim, who lives in Jacksonville, FL, had also called to say that he had read about my testimony and that I should call him. I returned all the calls, speaking to each for about fifteen minutes explaining how and why I had testified. All were surprised but were supportive of what I had done and hoped that it would all work out for the best. My brother had faxed me a clipping from the "Nation Briefing Section" of the *Jacksonville Times-Union* that referenced part of the conversation I had with the CNO on the patio pool area on Friday night.

Over the course of the next few days, I received several more calls and faxed clippings from different newspapers which cited my testimony. Then around 5:00 PM on Friday, Dec. 17, I answered my phone, and it was Robert Rae calling me from his law office in Norfolk. He told me that the hearing had concluded earlier and that the court was now in recess. He then spent a few minutes giving me a brief synopsis of what took place in the courtroom when first the prosecution followed by the defense teams presented their closing arguments.

As he had expected, Rae told me that I and my testimony were referred to by both sides' attorneys as well as Capt. Vest himself. When one of the prosecutors had reiterated to the judge that Adm. Kelso hadn't witnessed any inappropriate behavior at any time while at Tailhook, Capt. Vest cited my contrary testimony and asked how both statements could be true. The attorney answered by saying that I must be mistaken.

Later, when it was Rae's turn to present his conclusions, he told me that he recalled to Capt. Vest's attention the statements of several witnesses which refuted Adm. Kelso's claims. He specifically cited my testimony as being "irrefutable."

He told me he was optimistic about his clients' chances of being successful and said he expected that Capt. Vest would probably render his decision in four to six weeks. He thanked me again for stepping up and testifying. He told me that the entire defense team thought my testimony would play an important part in Capt. Vest's rulings. I thanked him for taking the time to call and told him I appreciated his kind words.

I wished him and all the defendants well and asked him to keep me in the loop if and when he heard anything from the judge about the decision. He said he would, and we exchanged our Merry Christmases.

During the next few weeks, there were several articles about Judge Vest's potential rulings and what may or may not happen. By in large, it was a quiet period until January 11 when the US Court of Military Appeals denied an appeal by another naval officer who attended Tailhook, Lt. David Samples, to dismiss the charges against him based on his belief that he had been granted immunity.[52] As a result, Mike Kmetz, Lt. Samples's attorney, petitioned Judge Vest to join the Tritt-Miller motion dismissing all his clients' charges. Capt. Vest eventually granted that petition. Soon thereafter, he made another ruling which surprised everyone. He pronounced that the prosecutor, LCDR Wayne Ritter, was disqualified from any further involvement in the case. This was the third such officer on the prosecution team whom Capt. Vest had dismissed, and it was seen, as yet, another significant blow to their team.

Four weeks later on Monday, February 7, I had just returned home from a three-day trip to Zurich, Switzerland, and back to Dulles. It had been a good trip—on time with a good crew. The weather in Zurich was perfect for sightseeing, and several of the crew got together and we spent the entire day exploring the beautiful city.

Now back in my home, I had unpacked, changed into dungarees and a sport shirt, grabbed a beer, and started going through my mail. I checked my answering machine, and the last message was from Robert Rae, which he left a few hours before. He told me that Judge Vest would make his ruling at 9:00 AM the next morning.

The stage was now set. In fifteen hours, everyone would find out what the future of the courts-martial of the three naval aviators would hold. For me personally, it would be an anxious night but considerably less so, I imagined, than for Tritt, Miller, and Samples.

Capt. Vest's Ruling and Its Effects

"I'm an honest man. I didn't lie, and I didn't manipulate the system."

THE WEATHER IN ANNAPOLIS ON Tuesday, February 8, 1994, was virtually identical to that in Norfolk, another city on the Chesapeake some 125 miles south: chilly, overcast, and windy. The Powers Courtroom inside the Norfolk Naval Legal Service Office was standing room only. The prosecution team was seated at a table on one side while the three defendants and their eight attorneys sat at three tables that had been joined together on the other side.

Promptly at 9:00 AM, Capt. Vest ordered the court to be in order. He explained that the motion before him was difficult and that he spent thousands of hours reviewing the trial record of 1,500 pages as well as hundreds of documents. He then read from page 111 of his "Essential Findings."[53] "It is hereby ordered, based on the findings of this court, that Adm. Kelso is an accuser within the meaning of Article 1(9), UCMJ, with regard to each accused and (2) that there has been both actual and apparent unlawful command influence in each case. The charges against Cdr. Thomas R. Miller, US Navy, Cdr. Gregory E. Tritt, US Navy, and Lt. David Samples, US Navy, are hereby *dismissed without prejudice* to the government's right to reinstate court-martial proceedings against the accused for the same offenses at a later date." He then disqualified Vice Adm. Paul Reason as the "convening authority" and allowed him to have three options as to what further actions he might take:

Take no further action against any or all of them effectively ending the proceedings;

Take administrative or nonjudicial disciplinary action in any or all of the cases in lieu of further judicial proceedings;

Forward the charges to an authority senior in rank to Adm. Kelso for disposition which might include reinstatement of charges against the three accused.

Capt. Vest then announced that Vice Adm. Reason had three days to make a decision as to which option he would choose. With that, he adjourned the hearing.

Later that afternoon around 4:00 PM, I received a phone call from Robert Rae who filled me in on what had transpired at the hearing. He described the court room scene upon learning of Judge Vest's rulings as one where all three defendants, their families, and defense teams were very emotional. Their initial reactions were a combination of thankfulness, relief, and hopefulness. I asked him what he thought would happen next, and he answered by saying that he thought Adm. Reason would probably choose to take no further action, thus ending this episode against Tritt, Miller, and Samples. Before we said good-bye to each other, he again thanked me for coming forward to help. He told me he was certain that my testimony had made a difference and that he would send me a copy of the ruling when things quieted down.

That evening, most national TV networks covered Capt. Vest's ruling. The next morning, the majority of newspapers had front-page stories as well.[54] Most of that coverage and that which took place over the next three days criticized either the CNO or the Navy establishment. Even though Judge Vest's ruling concerned highly technical pretrial legal issues, most commentators broadened their criticisms to either the Navy judicial system's inability to successfully prosecute the perpetrators of crimes or the Navy's leadership and its apparent complicity in a cover-up.

The announcement on Friday, February 13, by Vice Adm. Reason only further exacerbated the criticisms.[55] At a press conference at his Norfolk office, he announced that he had decided not to pursue further judicial actions against Tritt, Miller, and Samples, thus ending their prosecution as well as those of any of the remaining accused naval aviators who had attended Tailhook. While Adm. Reason's ruling no doubt pleased the three officers involved, their attorneys, families, and friends, there was one naval officer who was anything but pleased.

Adm. Kelso, the CNO, addressed the media later that day from his Pentagon office.[56] There was no disguising his anger and defiance as he spoke in front of the TV cameras. He adamantly denied doing anything wrong or improper at Tailhook. Further, he once again denied witnessing any improper or inappropriate behavior by anyone while he attended Tailhook. Lastly, he categorically denied doing anything improper or unethical as far as judicial procedures or UCMJ rules were concerned. He essentially told his media audience and its viewers that Judge Vest had gotten it completely wrong. He summed up his feelings when he said, "I'm an honest man. I didn't lie, and I didn't manipulate the system." Asked by reporters if he thought he might be forced to step down, he responded by saying, "I have no intention of resigning."

Clearly, Adm. Kelso had taken a position which suggested there was no wiggle room as far as his remaining in office until his scheduled retirement on June 30. However, the Secretary of the Navy, John H. Dalton, issued his own press release later that evening saying that he would spend time reviewing "the issues before me (which) are very complex."[57] He said that he would announce the results of his review of "how to proceed with Adm. Kelso in a week's time".

Over the next four days, there were, no doubt, high-level discussions between and among DoD and Navy officials as to how to proceed vis-à-vis Adm. Kelso. *New York Times* reporter Eric Schmitt was but one writer who had been following the Tailhook story and wrote that Secretary of Defense Perry and several of his department's high-ranking officials and Secretary of the Navy Dalton and his advisers had been intimately involved in negotiating the final outcome.[58]

The end result was that on February 15, at a Pentagon press conference, the CNO announced that he would be stepping down two months early in late April. "I clearly have become the lightning rod for Tailhook, and I think it's in the best interest of the Navy that if I proceed on and retire, we can get on with this business." He added that "I greatly regret that I did not have the foresight to be able to see that Tailhook could occur."

His announcement was accompanied by very supportive statements issued by both Secretary of Defense Perry and Secretary of the Navy Dalton. Perry essentially dismissed the very damning conclusions Judge Vest had reached against Adm. Kelso and unequivocally stated that "I regard Adm. Kelso as a man of the highest integrity and honor." For his part, Secretary of the Navy Dalton echoed the remarks of Perry, stating that the admiral "has acted as he has throughout his thirty-eight-year career, with the best interest of the United States Navy in mind." I couldn't help but think back to early October 1993 when I had read stories about Dalton's futile attempt to have Adm. Kelso "step down" as part of his plan to address Tailhook.[59] I'm certain that now SECNAV had also considered what might have been if he had been successful.

It was clear that SECDEF Perry had based his defense of Kelso almost entirely on the much criticized DoD IG investigation conducted by Derek J. Vander Schaaf even though its findings were in large measure disputed by most commentators. Indeed, that investigation was neither as thorough nor as focused as the testimony given under oath in Judge Vest's courtroom. In fact, many of the important "eye witnesses" who had testified in the courtroom had neither been contacted nor interviewed in the IG investigation.

The reaction to Adm. Kelso's early retirement announcement was as immediate as it was predictable. The political critics were especially outspoken regarding the latest deal which would leave another high-ranking naval officer unscathed from any punishment from Tailhook. While DoD and Navy officials might have thought that this would soon blow over and things would get back to normal, they were greatly mistaken. The opposing political forces would soon be reengaged, and this time, the battle would take place on the Senate floor as the entire Senate would soon vote on retiring Adm. Kelso as a four-star, thus allowing him his full annual pension of $84,000.

On Tuesday, April 19, it was a "battle royal" led on the one side by all the women of the Senate regardless of party affiliation who were against allowing Adm. Kelso to retire at full pension.[60] There was intense last-minute lobbying by the DoD and naval establishment. In the end, after six hours of an angry and heated debate, the vote was 54–43, approving the full retirement. In addition to the unanimous vote by the seven women senators, there were a number of republican male Senators who surprisingly joined the opposition. Among the mostly democratic Senators voting with the women in the minority were Senators Arlen Specter, Alfonse D'Amato, and Robert Packwood—strange bed fellows, for sure.

Many believed that the approval vote was a foregone conclusion because its passage had been brokered weeks before as part of the negotiations leading to Adm. Kelso's early retirement. While it might seem to have been a fait accompli, the opposition could also claim a victory of sorts—clearly a message from the Senate had been sent to the Armed Services about sexual harassment.

Four days later on April 23, Adm. Kelso formerly stepped down as the chief of Naval Operations in a ninety-minute change-of-command ceremony conducted at the Naval Academy in Annapolis, MD. Highlighting his thirty-eight-year naval career, Tailhook was only obliquely referred to. His successor as CNO was Adm. Jeremy M. Boorda who had been serving as the NATO military commander in Southern Europe. Of course, Adm. Boorda, whose previous assignment was as head of BUPERS was no stranger to Tailhook since it was he who had received Lt. Coughlin's initial accusation and who had, in effect, quickly ended the career of her boss at Pax River, Rear Adm. Jack Snyder.

While this change-of-command ceremony marked the end of Adm. Kelso's naval career, the woman officer who had initiated the Tailhook story, Lt. Paula Coughlin, would also soon be separated from the Navy. The media coverage of her resignation was mostly overshadowed by the Capt. Vest v. Adm. Kelso judicial rulings back in early February. It could hardly have been a mere coincidence that on the very same day, February 10, that Vice Adm. Reason issued his ruling ending the courts-martial and SECNAV Dalton released his statement about Adm. Kelso's future, Lt. Coughlin submitted her letter of resignation. In it, she said that her Tailhook assault "and the covert attacks on me that followed have stripped me of my ability to serve."[61] No doubt, the previous dismissal months before of the court-martial charges against her only identifiable assailant, Capt. Gregory Bonam, USMC, had also had a profound impact on her career choice as well. She was officially released from active duty on May 31, 1993.

While she no longer had an official relationship with the Navy, she continued to have a legal relationship with the Tailhook Association.[62] She and her attorneys successfully persisted in their litigation in Las Vegas courtrooms against the Tailhook Association, the Hilton Hotel Corporation, and the Las Vegas Hilton. A few days before the trial was set to begin, a tentative settlement was reached between Coughlin and the San Diego-based Tailhook Association on September 8, 1994. The *Las Vegas Review-Journal* reported that John Gormley, a lawyer for Tailhook, confirmed the agreed upon settlement but disclosed no details. After that agreement was reached, the Las Vegas US district court judge hearing the case, Philip Pro, had asked the attorneys representing Coughlin and Hilton Hotels to seek a mutually acceptable agreement, but a settlement was never reached.

On Monday, September 12, the jury trial began and lasted for seven weeks. At the core of the action was the assertion by Coughlin's attorneys that the Hilton failed to provide adequate security during the Tailhook symposium. They argued that there was negligence which led to emotional distress and sought both compensatory and punitive damages for their client. The testimony and evidence introduced resurrected all the inconsistencies, shortcomings, and inadequacies of the various reports and investigations to date. It also clearly shown a spotlight on the unacceptable behavior described in the most detailed, unflattering, and graphic language that had been going on for years at the annual gathering of naval aviators.

On October 28, 1994, the jury returned the verdict in favor of Paula Coughlin and against the Hilton Hotel Corporation and the Las Vegas Hilton for compensatory damages in the amount of $1.7 million—but that wasn't all. Three days later, on October 31, the jury returned a second verdict awarding Coughlin punitive damages in the amount of $5 million. Appeals were expected, and it didn't take very long for the first one to be settled. On March 9, 1995, Judge Pro reduced Coughlin's compensatory damages award. Revealing that Coughlin had previously received the undisclosed settlement from the Tailhook Association of $400,000, the judge subtracted that amount from her $1.7 million award. Further, he also reduced Coughlin's punitive damages award to $3.9 million. Thus, her total award from Hilton was reduced from $6.7 to $5.2 million. The Las Vegas Hilton and its parent, the Hilton Hotels Corporation, thereupon appealed that judgment; however, a three-person appellate court upheld both the decision and the award more than two years later on May 2, 1997, thus effectively ending the four-year litigious battle.

The resignations of these two major Tailhook figures, Adm. Kelso and Lt. Coughlin, were appropriately receiving significant coverage from the media. The naval establishment and especially the aviation community were necessarily closely following these ongoing stories. Meanwhile, there were many more naval officers whose careers were also ending, but their individual stories went essentially unnoticed by everyone. *One of them was mine!*

During this same time period of resignations in 1994, I was acutely aware that my own naval career might soon be coming to a critical juncture as the results of the "Reserve Rear Admiral [Lower Half] Selection Board" would be announced any day. As this was the year which I believed I had the best opportunity to be promoted from my current rank of captain to rear admiral, I had thoroughly reviewed my official records at BUPERS for accuracy and completeness and was satisfied that everything was in order. Because I had the experience of being a member of several promotion boards in the previous seven years, I thought I had a well-informed opinion as to what a promotable record looked like.

Navy selection (promotion) boards are made up exclusively of officers who are of the next higher rank than those who are being selected. So in my case, the rank of the officers on the board was rear admiral (one star) with the sole exception that the president is usually a vice admiral (three stars). A typical selection board meets for five to fifteen days, depending on the number of records involved, at BUPERS which is located about a mile south of the Pentagon. In this case, it was scheduled to be a seven-day board. The process begins with the record of each officer in the promotion zone being reviewed in detail by one member of the board. After a certain number are reviewed, the board members then go into and take their assigned seats in a mini theatre called the "tank." In seniority order, an officer's record is then displayed on the three screens and the officer who reviewed that particular record then "briefs" it. He (or she) verbally reviews the record, pointing out salient points which he believes are significant or noteworthy. At the end of the brief which typically takes two to five minutes, every board member casts a secret vote using a handheld electronic device. The box allows for a member to vote either Yes or No, and if Yes, to assign a specific confidence number, i.e., 25%, 50%, 75%, or 100%. When all members have entered their votes, the final tally is automatically calculated and shown so that all can see the resultant score. (As an example, if there were fifteen board members, the extremes of the vote would be fifteen Yeses and 100%—a perfect score. On the other end would be fifteen Nos and 0%).

After the total population of records gets evaluated, then the board sees a graphic hierarchal breakdown of the scores. The board then begins a voting process involving the approving and disapproving of records depending on their scores. As this willowing process proceeds, second, third, and sometimes fourth additional reviews and briefs of records by different board members are required to finally arrive at the predetermined number of officers to be selected.

It never ceased to amaze me how time consuming, sometimes tedious and difficult, this process was. But most importantly, it was generally accepted to be the fairest system yet devised. I had been on a lieutenant commander, commander, and three captain selection boards, and I had left them all with the same exhausted but rewarding feeling. While I may have, at times, felt that someone I thought whose record qualified him to be promoted but wasn't, I always felt that everyone who was selected deserved to be. At times, a board member's individual bias and partiality were evident during the "brief" of an officer's record, but most overlooked this shortcoming and voted just on the record alone. This is not to say that a briefer had no effect on the outcome of the vote. Indeed, like in any other selling-type endeavor, the skill of the seller may very well be the difference in whether an individual gets selected or not. This is especially the case in the area that is commonly referred to as the "crunch." After those at the top are selected and those at the bottom are deselected, it then comes down to perhaps subtle and seemingly insignificant issues that will separate those to be selected from those who will not. It is in this arena where the skill of a briefer might be the critical factor. No doubt, everyone who has ever served on a selection board has witnessed this experience and, like me, comes away hoping that, if their own record is ever in the crunch, a skilled briefer who would become your advocate will be assigned.

One spring morning after I returned home after having breakfast with the "boys" at Jim's Corner, I received a call from a Naval Reserve friend of mine. He was currently performing his annual two-week active duty obligation at the Navy IG office where I had recently commanded the reserve unit. He told me he had been reviewing the latest message traffic and had just finished reading an ALNAV(all Navy) message that announced the FY 95 Reserve Rear Admiral (lower half) selectees. Because he too was a naval aviator, he focused his attention on the 1315 (naval aviator designator) selectees as those represented the community that both of us were in. Normally, of the thirteen total rear admiral selectees, two would be aviators: one from the TACAIR (Tailhook and helicopter) community and one from the Patrol/Transport community.

With some reticence, he told me that he had hoped that my name would be on the list, but it wasn't. He said he had thought about not calling me and thus avoid being the bearer of bad news, but thought that if the roles had been reversed, he'd want a close friend like me to break the news. I asked him to tell me the names of the aviators selected, and he read me both names. I didn't recognize the gent who represented the patrol community, but I was very familiar with the officer who represented my own TACAIR community. He and I were contemporaries who had similar active duty and reserve careers as Tailhookers. Our paths had crossed many times over the previous fifteen years, and I knew he had an excellent reputation as well as a record of accomplishments especially in those important commanding officer billets which he had when he was both a commander and captain.

We chatted for a few minutes then signed off. Before I did, I thanked him for making the call even though it was not good news. I sat for a while contemplating what I had just heard. I was certainly disappointed but not surprised that I didn't make the cut. My first thought was that the selection board must have come to the conclusion that that my record was either not good enough or was not as good as the gent who was ultimately selected. In either case, the result was the same. No one on this selection board was as familiar as I with my record. I realized that if it came down to my service record being in the crunch, there was one fitness report interspersed among the many I had received over my twenty-eight-year career that was somewhat less than all the other outstanding ones I had received from my superior officers. There was little doubt in my mind that if a briefer focused the board's attention in a negative light on this shortcoming, it might just be the kiss of death.

I also considered the possibility that my role in the courts-marshal hearings might have had a bearing on the selection process. It was now part of the established promotion process for active duty officers that the service records of any one known to have attended Tailhook would be "flagged"—i.e., they would be pulled and scrutinized to make certain that there was nothing derogatory or accusatory in the various investigative reports. This "extra" step had been mandated by the SASC (Senate Armed Services Committee). I was unaware if this procedure had also been the case with reserve promotions, but I didn't think it mattered in my case because I had never been mentioned in any of the investigative reports. True, my name and my participation at Tailhook had made headlines and I, personally, had been the subject of comments by the CNO, Adm. Kelso, and his staff as well as the prosecutors in the court-marshal. Yet I found it difficult to believe that any of this could have found its way into the selection process—that is, until days later, when an associate of mine who was a member of the selection board called me.

He explained that the briefer of my record whom I had known for a long time did me no favors in reviewing my record to his fellow board members. He seemed to focus on the one less than outstanding fitrep (fitness report) almost to exclusion of any other part of my record. When he was done briefing and the vote taken, it was apparent to all that my selection was impossible. My friend asked me if there had been any bad blood issues between us. I responded that many years before when we were both squadron commanding officers in the same reserve air wing, we did have some serious disagreeable words together—"But that was more than twelve years ago," I said.

There was no suitable comment I could think of, so we concluded the phone conversation.

One day much later, I thought about that conversation with my friend and my past history with my "briefer" and recalled, in addition to our little brouhaha, that it was well-known that he had had a close personal relationship with Adm. Kelso as they were both proud "Southern gentlemen." Then, as now, it would indeed be interesting to find out conclusively if my testimony had played any part in my nonselection. Regardless, I now had to face the question of whether I should remain in the Naval Reserves for another year so as to be considered by the next year's selection board.

After a good deal of soul-searching and many discussions with friends and especially with Stefanie, I decided in June to submit my resignation request effective September 30, 1994. The choice was not easy because there were many important factors to be considered. In the end, I believed the time had come for me to pack it in and move on. I had a wonderful run of more than thirty-two years of service. There was only one last naval obligation to undertake. It was now time to plan a suitable retirement ceremony.

My Final Naval Cruise

"It all began in Sheepshead Bay. Little Bobby Beck had gone fishing that day."

SOON AFTER SUBMITTING MY RESIGNATION papers, I started to think about past retirement ceremonies that I had attended, trying to imagine what I wanted mine to look like. Unfortunately, the very memorable ones involved active-duty officers who had many advantages over their Reserve counterparts when it came to "puttin' on the dog." Nowhere was this disparity more apparent than when a Navy ship, especially a supercarrier, was used as the backdrop.

Throughout my career, I had been a very proud witness to many change of command, retirement, christening, commissioning, and decommissioning ceremonies aboard aircraft carriers. In my opinion, no other function-military or civilian-can match the pomp and circumstance that such an event entails. As much as I would have loved to have my ceremony on a "big deck," I knew there was no way I could make it happen if for no other reason than logistically the event had to take place near Annapolis. I had even entertained the idea of having it aboard the USS *Barry, DD-933*, docked at the Washington Navy Yard which is the US Navy's oldest shore establishment. However, I soon dismissed this because I knew that many of my Annapolis friends would not be very receptive to the inconvenience of having to make the round-trip drive to DC on a weekend afternoon in September. Additionally, the fact was, if I couldn't have it on a carrier, there was no good reason to have it on any other vessel.

At that point, Stef came up with an inspired idea. A few months earlier, while we were enjoying a walk around the Naval Academy Yard, she and I had visited the Robert Crown Sailing Center located on the bank of the Severn River adjacent to the Santee Basin where the Academy's sailing fleet is moored. Stefanie remembered that the top floor of the modern looking building had a wonderful large room which she thought might be an ideal setting for the event. So the next afternoon, we revisited the building and talked to the receptionist about the feasibility of using the second floor room for a retirement ceremony. We were excited to learn that it was possible and learned how to go about reserving the room.

I had envisioned having a typical Navy informal program where I would welcome everyone and then introduce the honored speaker. Following that, I would then give my speech. After the ceremony, there would be food and beverages for a one- to two-hour reception. For weeks, Stef and I went over all the details of the guest list, invitations, times and date, food and beverages, parking, etc. Even though everything was falling into place, we both agreed that the ceremony lacked "pizzazz." She then had an epiphany. "Why not go all out and really do it up big and retire in style on a presidential vessel?" It just so happened that one of our close friends, Roger Kolasinski, owned such a yacht, conveniently docked in Annapolis and available for hire.

El Presidente is an historic ninety-six-foot 1939 Mathis-Trumpy motor yacht. Originally named *Innisfall* and built for the J. M. Cudahy family, she was a pleasure craft which primarily cruised the United States east coast for the next several years. During WWII, she was pressed into service by the US Navy and was refitted in Philadelphia in 1942 and was commissioned as YP-354. She served as a coastal patrol boat for five years with her two 20 mm cannons on deck and her depth charge rack on her stern. After the war, she was decommissioned and refurbished but remained in government service. Her guests included eight US presidents, countless foreign dignitaries, and many heads of state. After Roger acquired her, he personally supervised her refit and rehabilitation, which brought her back to her exalted status as one of the most graceful and elegant "Great Gatsby" era yachts still in existence.

In talking with Roger and trying to fit my event into his ship's schedule, it became clear that it was going to be difficult since weekend bookings were in high demand. Fortunately for me, Roger generously carved out a three-hour period in the early afternoon of Saturday, September 24. This was the final and most important piece of the ceremony. The guest list had to be reworked and reduced to seventy-five to be in compliance with Coast Guard capacity requirements. In the meantime, I had received confirmation from my two admiral buddies—Jack Moriarty and Jay Miller—that they would be attending as my guests of honor. The room at the sailing center would be set up for seventy-five seats at 11:00 AM. Stefanie had made arrangements for local caterers to supply and serve on board the food and beverages she had carefully selected. A month to go and every detail save one—the weather—had been painstakingly addressed.

My final weekend duty with my Naval Reserve unit in Norfolk took place two weeks before my formal retirement ceremony. I had driven down to Norfolk Naval Base from Annapolis on Friday night arriving at the BOQ at midnight. I had been kept busy all day Saturday and Sunday completing all my assignments and helping the officer who was my relief to understand the duties he was about to inherit after I retired. I had just finished the last details of my pass-down duties before the start of our scheduled "all-hands" meeting, which took place a little sooner than normal. At 4:00 PM on all Sunday afternoons, the seventy officers and petty officers would gather in an auditorium to hear presentations from the department heads, the executive, and commanding officers. Normally, this would take about a half hour after which everyone would be dismissed and soon thereafter leave for home.

On this particular afternoon, however, we met earlier at 3:30 PM. The briefings all went as usual until toward the end of the CO's talk. He normally concluded with his plans for the next month's drill weekend and then dismissed the unit personnel. This time he delivered his plans, but then instead of dismissing us, he asked me to join him up on stage. While standing next to him, he described my thirty-two-year naval career in very complimentary terms for the next several minutes. He then read a letter of commendation addressed to me from the head of our active duty gaining command, CINCLANT (commander-in-chief, Atlantic). I was very touched both by the speech and the letter. After he concluded, he offered me the microphone, and I told him how much I appreciated his kind gesture. I told everyone that I was honored to have been part of such a wonderful group of people for the last year. I wished that all of them would have as rewarding career as I had and could be associated with as many fantastic people as well.

When I was finished, everyone stood up and applauded. I was very moved by all this. Afterward, a retirement cake, ice cream, and beverages were served. Many of my shipmates came over to congratulate me, and a few even commented on my court-martial testimony almost a year earlier and said how proud they were to have known me. For me, it was a very humbling experience.

The last person I talked to was my CO, and I thanked him for doing all this for me. "It was," I told him, "above and beyond and I will be forever grateful." The four-hour drive back to my Annapolis home, though long, was very enjoyable because the time allowed me to think how lucky I had been all these years.

The next two weeks literally and figuratively "flew by" as I travelled to European cities three times in just eleven days. Before I realized it, I was driving to the airport to pick up my Mom, Kay, and my younger brother, Jim, who had flown up from Tampa and Jacksonville, respectively. Both arrived early on Friday morning and would be staying at my home with Stef and me.

My two admiral "guests of honor" buddies had also flown in on Friday and had already made their way to the homes of their Annapolis hosts—Fred and Luke. They would be their roomies until Sunday. Later that day, many of us gathered at Fred's house, which is about twenty-five yards from McGarvey's for predinner cocktails. By the time we finally managed to talk our way out of Fred's, the group had swelled to about fifteen, and I had only made reservations for eight. At 8:00 PM, the saloon was standing room only but lucky for us the manager was on duty, and I explained to Jimmy that our group had expanded considerably. Before he left us at the bar, he asked that I give him ten minutes to make arrangements, so naturally we all ordered drinks and started "shooting the bull" with more of our friends seated at the front bar.

I was barely into a conversation about tomorrow's activities with a couple of my friends when Jimmy came over and told me that the Aviator Room was all set up for us. The next three hours were filled with mostly aviation and sailing stories, which all seemed to end with belly laughs from everyone. Around 11:00 PM, I guessed that my mom was getting restless, so when most of the gang was heading back to Fred's place for a nightcap, we took our leave and headed back home.

Early the next morning, we thankfully awoke to a beautiful day, and the weather report was ideal for an afternoon boat ride on Chesapeake. Stef and I stayed busy for the next few hours as we ensured that the arrangements were all completed. The four of us arrived at the sailing center at 10:15 AM and were happy to see that everything was in order. By 11:00 AM, all the guests were seated.

As I stood at the podium, I could hardly believe the gathering that I was looking at: my mom and brother, my girlfriend, my Academy roommate and a couple of classmates, some longtime Navy buddies, many members of the 912 squadron, some sailing and motorcycle friends, fellow ex-Eastern and United pilots, and a bunch of fellow Annapolitans. It was almost too good to be true!

The next forty-five minutes went by too quickly. Jack's and Jay's speeches were as good as the best I had ever heard. They reminded me of so many memorable events that I had witnessed with them during the years when we had flown together. When it was my turn to speak, I thanked my lucky stars that I had decided days before to write more than just an outline of my speech. I was very nervous but was pretty sure that I had included everyone in the audience in my story which I told them and the important part that each had played in my life.

Afterward, everyone met at the city dock about a mile away and boarded the *El Presidente*. She looked incredible, and all the landlubbers who were standing on the city docks waved at us as we left the harbor and headed toward the Severn River and the Bay. While everybody was eating and drinking and enjoying the cruise, I went over to Stefanie and told her I couldn't believe how great this had turned out. It was certainly among the best events I had ever attended. After being at sea for an hour or so, I was invited out on the fantail where everyone had gathered. Some of my friends presented me with gifts while others had given little speeches in my honor. Finally, Stefanie called me to her side and proceeded to read the poem about my life which she had written:

"It all began in Sheepshead Bay. Little Bobby Beck had gone fishing that day, when lo and behold overhead an airplane flew, and right then he knew, an Aviator was what he wanted to be, and to Mom and Dad he said, 'I'll do it. You'll see.'"

The poem, which had many more verses, seemed to capture the major points in my life in a wonderful manner. I was totally taken aback—it was a most rewarding and humbling experience. I thanked Stef and everyone for honoring me by attending my retirement ceremony. As I was finishing, almost on cue, all of us could hear the unique roar of radial engines, and we looked up and saw three *Warbird SNJ* aircraft. Most of the aviators present had learned how to fly different versions of these planes, which were used by both the Air Force and Navy in their primary flight schools. As the three planes came around for another low-pass, I recognized the lead plane as one owned by an American Airlines captain friend of mine Andy Mickalak. It was decked out in an award-winning Maryland Air National Guard paint scheme and looked like it was brand-new. After making a few more passes, they departed, and Fred told me that Andy and his wingmen were returning from a *Warbirds* fly-in and had prearranged the timing of their private air show to coincide with the yacht cruising in the middle of the bay. It was a grand performance that was the perfect ending to the onboard ceremony.

Ending such a spectacular cruise as this, especially with your close friends, is always a sad affair, but ending this one was particularly depressing. If we could no longer be on the water, at least we could continue to party—so many of us headed back to the saloon to keep the celebration going. Mike was the perfect host over the next few hours while all of us were being entertained listening to so many personal tales recounted by expert storytellers.

The last conversation I had before we left was a very meaningful one with my ex-Stinger roommate and companion at Tailhook '91, Jack Moriarty. We discussed how the lives and careers of so many of our aviator comrades had been forever changed by Tailhook. Even though Jack had retired two years before on October 1, 1992, he was, nevertheless, one of the thirty admirals who had received a nonpunitive letter of caution from SECNAV Dalton a year later in October 1993.

Jack's last assignment had been as commander, Strike/Fighter Wings, Atlantic based at Naval Air Station Cecil Field, Jacksonville, Florida. In this tour of duty, he was in charge of virtually all F/A-18 Hornet assets based on the East Coast. Jack's entire military profession had well prepared him for this important assignment.

His career which began as a Massachusetts Maritime Academy graduate witnessed a remarkable succession of operational billets. He had first flown the venerable AD-1 "Spad," then the A-7E Corsair II, and then finally, the F/A-18 Hornet. Because he had graduated from the US Naval Test Pilot School, he had also accumulated flight time in a wide variety of other naval aircraft, including the F-8 Crusader. He had commanded VA-46, an A-7E squadron and VA-122, the A-7 Master Training Squadron on the West Coast. He had been the executive officer of the USS *Coral Sea* and the commanding officer of the USS *John F. Kennedy.* He had logged more than one thousand carrier landings—an accomplishment attained only by a very few naval aviators.

As disappointed as I was about ending my Reserve career sooner than I had wished, I felt far worse for Jack and all the other active-duty admirals whose careers had ended prematurely simply because they had attended Tailhook '91. For many, their post-Navy careers were likewise adversely affected as well because of the stigma of the letters and the adverse publicity of Tailhook. Although Jack seemed to have reluctantly accepted the end of his career, I was deeply upset that the Navy and the country had lost the services of such a dedicated, talented, and devoted leader. It wasn't even close to being fair, but like both of us used to say, "It's the breaks of Naval Air."

Since Jack would be leaving early the next morning, we said our good-byes right before I left the saloon. I thanked him for coming up from Florida and told him how honored I was to have him as a close friend. Attending my retirement had resulted in this being a bitter-sweet occasion for both of us. As I walked away with my mom and Stef each holding an arm, my thoughts were of my favorite wartime movie quote: "Where do we find such men?"—the penultimate line from *The Bridges at Toko-Ri.*

Three Reunions in 2011

"Make us proud."

Pensacola, May 2011

EVERY YEAR SINCE 1986, THE F-8 Crusader Association had celebrated their Last Annual Crusader Ball (LACB) usually at various military installations either in California or Texas. The fraternal organization's members were aviators who had flown the single-seat, single-engine supersonic aircraft built by the Vought Aircraft Company and first flown in 1955. The plane and the men who flew them amassed a distinguished and colorful record, which included the photo RF-8 taking pictures of Russian IRBMs in Cuba in the fall of 1962 and the fighter version attaining a 19:3 kill ratio against MIG aircraft in Vietnam. Two of its more famous nickname were the "Last of the Gunfighters" and the "MiG Master."

In 2010, the leadership of the organization had decided to have the twenty-fifth reunion take place in May 2011 in Pensacola, Florida, in conjunction with the naval air station's hosting its celebration of the one hundredth anniversary of Naval Aviation. As Pensacola was where all naval aviators began their flying career, it was a very special place to all who eventually received their "Wings of Gold." Thinking that this was going to be an exceptional opportunity, I thought that if there were ever a time for my previous RF-8 squadron, VFP-206, to have a reunion, this seemed to me to be the ideal venue. In January 2011, I began discussing the idea with my pal "Jbird" Miller and a couple of other friends who had served with me. They agreed that it should be done, and so we began to organize the effort to locate the pilots of the two Naval Air Reserve photo reconnaissance squadrons which had been colocated at NAF Washington at Andrews Air Force Base in the '70s and '80s. Over the next three months, I and others were able to contact just about every one of the pilots and staff officers and got many of them to sign up.

I had intended to fly my VFR-only experimental plane from West Palm Beach to Pensacola on Tuesday morning, May 3, 2011. Unfortunately, the weather was not especially inviting, so I had to drive the six hundred miles which took eight and half hours. I arrived at the hotel where most of the F-8 guys, and their wives, were staying at 5:00 PM. After I checked in, I met Jbird, and we went to the hospitality suite where the F-8 organization was located. After getting my badge, instructions, and goody bag, we grabbed beers and started meeting old friends. It never ceased to amaze me how easily and quickly all of the gang reconnected after so many years of separation.

The next morning Jay and I watched the Blue Angels perform a practice show over the air station and then participated in the golf tournament. As this was a Naval Air Symposium event, most golfers were aviators but only a few were F-8 guys. While enjoying the happy hour afterward, I had several conversations with Academy classmates as well as former A-7 drivers.

Later that evening, about thirty members of the two Washington based RF-8 squadrons met for dinner at Peg Leg Pete's Bar. I had arranged this get-together on Pensacola Beach, which was the scene of countless parties we all attended during our flight school days. For hours, we enjoyed the good old times and got reacquainted with comrades some of whom we hadn't seen in more than twenty years.

The next day was spent attending several events of the Naval Air Symposium which were fascinating. Sessions One and Two addressed the development of Naval Air from its beginning in 1911 to the end of the Vietnam War. In one presentation, David Hartman (the first host of *Good Morning America*) was the moderator of a panel of four well-known naval aviators one of whom I knew very well. Capt. "Hap" Chandler was "a fighter pilot's fighter pilot" who witnessed Japanese kamikaze attacks in WWII. He was also a member of one of the most exclusive groups in Naval Air: the Four C's Club. Its aviators had flown all four of the famous Vought aircraft—the F-4U, Corsair; the F-7U Cutless; the F-8 Crusader; and the A-7 Corsair II. Finally, he was one of the most revered commanding officers of Miramar, "Fightertown USA." During his memorable tenure as CO in the early '70s, I had dated one of his daughters. After his talk on stage, I met him and his wife and chatted about times past. Reuniting with him was quite an unexpected pleasure.

Later that evening, I attended the formal symposium reception and banquet, which was the main social event of the week-long festivities. Again, I was reunited with squadron mates, USNA classmates and colleagues I hadn't seen in decades. A highlight of the evening was listening to the talk given by Adm. Tim Keating, who had recently retired from the Navy having served as head of PACOM (Pacific Command). I had known "Timbo" since my NAS Lemoore days in the seventies and had been fortunate to cross paths with him at various times during his distinguished career. His speech about the important role of Naval Aviation in the history of our nation was as captivating and as interesting as any speech I've ever heard. Before I headed back to my hotel, I sought him out and was fortunate to spend a few minutes "yuking it up" with my brother attack pilot and LSO.

I spent all Friday morning walking throughout the museum buildings on a guided tour conducted by an eighty-five-year-old retired naval aviator volunteer. As he was a Tailhooker, he gave us the cook's tour, and it was fantastic. I have been to many aviation museums all over the world, but this was something very, very special. I literally saw, and touched, just about every plane in the Navy inventory—including all those I personally had flown.

After lunch, I met Jay, and we attended the concluding event, which was the flag panel. Like that of the Tailhook symposium, it was composed of the leaders of Naval and Marine Aviation. Watching members of the "Old Guard" criticize the policies and politics of this "new Navy" brought smiles to our faces. We were both greatly impressed with the questions and comments coming from the JOs and student naval aviators (SNAs). All in all, I was happy that I had attended this session.

We got back to our hotel and had a drink in the hospitality suite before we changed into coat and tie and attended the Twenty-Fifth Last Annual Crusader Ball. After cocktail hour, the pilots of 206 and 306 sat together at dinner which was attended by more than three hundred "Sader" jocks. It was another fabulous event, which was filled with stories and remembrances about the "good old days of wooden ships and iron men." Many of these gents who were F-8 legends and had become my heroes for what they had done as pilots were appropriately recognized. Arguably, the most famous attendee was Tom Hudner, a retired Navy captain. During the Korean War, as a Corsair pilot, he had crash-landed his plane in enemy territory in order to rescue his wingman, Ens. Jesse Brown, the first African American naval aviator. Hudner was unsuccessful in retrieving him and was later picked up by a helicopter and returned to his carrier. For his extraordinary heroism, he was awarded the Medal of Honor. This story was the basis of William Holden's final scene in *The Bridges at Toko-Ri.*

The four days in Pensacola went by way too quickly, but I realized how much fun I had being surrounded with comrades-in-arms. On my drive back to West Palm Beach the next morning, I started to formulate a plan to further reengage the Naval Air scene by attending Tailhook 2011 in Reno in September. It would be the twentieth anniversary of attending my last one—Tailhook '91.

Reno, September 2011

Soon after we were married in November 1999, Stefanie and I purchased our summer home in Quogue, NY. It is a small and quiet historic residential village located on Long Island's south shore in the Hamptons. In all my travels, I have not come across a place with so many advantages as this gem. The carefree lifestyle, the friendliness of the people, the beauty of the land and beaches, and the wonderful climate make it an ideal place to live especially from May to October.

And then there are the area's spectacular golf courses that make this a paradise for those of us who daily like to "chase the white ball."

The months of June, July, and August were filled with memorable times with good friends enjoying the many benefits of retirement. My plans to attend the Fifty-Fifth Annual Tailhook Convention on September 8–11 had been completed, but with only two weeks to go, there was a major problem which might prevent me from travelling to Reno, Nevada. My right sciatic nerve was so severely inflamed by a herniated disc that I was essentially lame and in constant pain. My orthopedic doctor friend prescribed a seven-day steroid treatment plan that I began a week before my scheduled departure date.

That day arrived, Wednesday, September 7, but soon after I got up, I realized that it would be impossible for me to handle the trip. As I was flying standby "nonrev" on United, it wasn't a problem cancelling today's booking and relisting on a flight the next day. The real obstacle was that all Thursday nonstop flights from JFK to San Francisco were so heavily booked that my chances were slim on getting on a flight.

I got to the terminal at Kennedy in time to standby for the 11:00 AM flight which had a few empty seats, but they were eventually filled by revenue passengers. This identical procedure repeatedly happened on the next four flights. Luckily, my name was called at the very end of the boarding process for the 6:30 PM flight, which was the last departure of the night. As I walked down the ramp and onto the 757, I couldn't wait to get to my seat because the pain would be significantly less than when I was standing or walking. As I tried to find a comfortable position, I wondered if this trip were going to be worth the effort. We then experienced an hour "gate hold" before we took off and were rerouted enroute to San Francisco. We, thus, arrived hours late, and though I hustled as best I could, I was unable to make the last United flight to Reno. I took advantage of the twenty-four-hour US Servicemen's hospitality room at the airport and spent five hours in a lounge chair trying to get some sleep.

At 9:00 AM, I managed to get on a flight to Reno and eventually got to the Silver Legacy Hotel where many other Tailhookers were staying. After a quick shower, shave and change of clothes, I got a van ride over to the Nugget, which had hosted the symposium for the previous sixteen years. Although I had missed the "Winging" ceremony of two Navy and two Marine officers conducted by my friend Tim Keating, I was in time for the "Evaluation of Carrier Aircraft" presentation. I recognized most of the distinguished panel who were experts of aircraft flown from WW II to the present day. It was an interesting and informative talk given by people who were knowledgeable about many of the most famous and revered carrier aircraft.

From 4:30 to 6:00 PM, I hobbled, in pain, through the exhibition hall where all seventy-five different defense contractors, vendors, and other associations had set up their displays and booths. Many had very sophisticated computer shows and *Star Wars*–type simulations that were mind-boggling as to capabilities. And, of course, I collected some mementoes which I would soon add to my Tailhook collection. I started making my way back to the ballroom area to attend the "Bug" Roach memorial Flight-Deck Mixer. Some four thousand aviators, many dressed in their official and "Sierra Hotel" (Shit Hot) flight suits and guests participated in this cocktail-hour event. It was the closest thing to the happy hours at Naval Air Station officers' clubs, which I regularly attended during my active-duty years. For almost four hours, it was a real treat hanging out with old friends, meeting and talking with the new breed of JOs and "counseling" many SNAs. By the time I returned to my room at 11:00 PM, I was more than exhausted and ready for the rack.

I arrived back at the Nugget Late on Saturday morning and attended the last two of the three scheduled panel discussions: "Naval Aviation Warriors" moderated by Tim Keating and "Aviation Flag Panel" moderated by Vice Adm. Al Myers, commander, Naval Air Forces. I was captivated listening to all the men during both sessions, but my favorite was the man whom I had only said hello to back in Pensacola, Capt. Tom Hudner, the Corsair and Crusader pilot who received the Medal of Honor. For me, it was a boyhood dream come true to listen to him explain, in detail, his fateful mission in Korea firsthand.

After changing clothes back at my hotel, I returned at 6:00 PM to the predinner cocktail party where more than two thousand guests attended the formal banquet. At 7:30 PM, we were seated and the dinner began. The remaining three prestigious awards were presented to the best carrier/air wing team, the Marine Corps Tailhooker of the Year and the Navy Tailhooker of the Year. As the desserts were being served, the outgoing president of the Tailhook Association, Capt. Jay Campbell, introduced the guest speaker, Sen. John McCain. I was anticipating an entertaining and insightful speech and was not disappointed. Its theme was leadership, and his talk was well received by the appreciative audience. As good as it was, I was somewhat dismayed when he made the point that in today's "politically correct" Navy, many of the best leaders in the past would not have made it past the current "one strike and you're out" policy. In light of his crucial role in the Tailhook '91 debacle, I could not reconcile his two conflicting positions. His concluding plea to the JOs was to "make us proud." After receiving a standing ovation, the M/C pronounced that the dinner was over. I stayed in the ballroom for a while talking to friends who had been seated at other tables and then left to get the van back to my hotel. On the way out, I saw three young naval aviators sitting at the bar and decided I needed "one for the ditch." I spent the next hour chatting with them about Sen. McCain's speech and their reactions to it. As I was leaving them, I thanked them for their service and wished them well in their careers as naval aviators. "Have fun," were my last words as I walked out of the bar on my way to the van.

The next morning, I checked in and got on a United flight to Denver. As we had an early arrival and the connecting gate was close by, I was just barely in time to catch a flight to LaGuardia just as the agent was closing out the flight. She escorted me down the jetway and closed the door behind me as I walked aboard. The best part, so far, was that I had been assigned the last empty seat in first class. I relaxed immediately and the pain in my right leg seemed to almost go away.

A couple of cocktails and a good meal later, I started to scan some of the literature I had acquired. I was looking at the September issue of the Naval Institute *Proceedings*, which was celebrating the Naval Aviation centennial. One article especially caught my eye: "Is Naval Aviation Culture Dead?" by John Lehman. "Holy crap," I said to myself. What a strange coincidence, the thrust of his article was essentially identical to the speech delivered just hours before by Sen. McCain. While I agreed with many of his points which had to do with the aftermath of Tailhook '91, I couldn't agree with his assessment that "the mindless pursuit of zero-tolerance" will lead to an organization that will fail. In light of the discussions I just had with JOs and learning about how they viewed their profession and careers, I was as enthusiastic as I could be about their future and that of Naval Air. I vowed that if I had the chance, I would further discuss this with John the next time our paths crossed.

After arrival at LaGuardia, I took the subway to Long Island Railroad Jamaica Station and then took the LIRR to Ronkonkoma where I had parked my car. One more forty-minute drive and I'd finally be home. It had been about eleven hours since I left my hotel in Reno and in spite of the difficulties associated with flying standby and the sciatic pain I endured, attending Tailhook '11 had been well worth the effort.

New York City, November 2011

Now back in our condo in West Palm Beach in late October, I received a phone call from Mary Lou McCann, a close friend married to Jim who is the CEO of 1-800-Flowers. She asked if Stefanie and I would join them as their guests attending the Princess Grace Awards Gala on November 1, 2011, in New York City. As Stef wasn't at home, I thanked Mary Lou for the invitation and told her I was confident that Stef would love to go and that she could reach her on her cell phone. A short time later, Stef called me and said that she just talked to Mary Lou and had accepted their invitation. She was ecstatic—literally jumping with joy anticipating a great time at the black tie affair.

Later that night, I got on the computer to research the Princess Grace Foundation as well as the awards gala. I was happy to learn that my friend John Lehman remained as the foundation's chairman and that he would be the gala's MC. Further, I learned that the award's dinner would take place at Cipriani's on Forty-Second Street directly across from Grand Central Station. Formerly the Bowery Savings Bank, "this Italian Renaissance inspired masterpiece showcases towering marble columns, soaring ceilings, magnificent inlaid floors and glorious chandeliers," is how this venue is described on the Cipriani's Web site. As I surveyed the many beautiful photographs, I was getting more excited by the minute.

I soon e-mailed both John and my Annapolis buddy, Mike Ashford, telling them that Stefanie and I would be attending as guests of the McCanns' and hoped we'd be able to get together with them at the event. It was easy to remember John's history with the foundation as he was the cousin of Princess Grace. On the other hand, Mike had attended several previous dinners with John and I had my fingers crossed that we three former shipmates would soon be partying in the Big Apple. John soon responded that he was looking forward to getting together, but Mike called to tell me that he had other plans. I was disappointed that I wouldn't see the captain, but I was delighted to know that both John and Barbara, his wife, would be there. I also asked John if Prince Albert would be there because I was hoping that he and I would be reunited after forty-one years. As both the Prince and his wife would indeed be there, I was now very eager to attend the event.

A couple of weeks later, we were in New York walking the few blocks from our hotel to Cipriani's on a beautiful and mild fall evening. The entrance to the building had a huge crowd, photographers, and a red carpet as well. Inside the room was decked out to the nines. Soon we met and were having cocktails with Jim and Mary Lou and their four other guests. We were soon called to our seats and then listened to John deliver his opening remarks. After he had completed, Stefanie and I walked over to a nearby table where he was engaged in lively conversations with several guests. He turned around and smiled at us after he heard me call his name. He and Barbara, Stef and I spoke for a few minutes about the good old times, and then John accompanied us back to our table where I introduced him to Mary Lou, Jim, and our other table guests.

After John left, I then recognized Prince Albert standing in a crowd not far away and suggested to Stef that this might be a good time for her to approach the prince with her story. Stefanie was up and away before I had a chance to remind her of the details but was comfortable that she would do just fine. It didn't take much for Stefanie to convince the prince's bodyguard why she needed to be able to talk to him so that he let her approach the prince of Monaco. Stef asked the prince if, as a young boy, he remembered being escorted by a young naval officer on a day tour on the aircraft carrier, USS *Saratoga*, which was cruising the Mediterranean off the French coast in 1970. Stefanie told me later that his face was lighting up and at the end of her question, he answered, "Yes, of course, I remember the *Saratoga* and its airplanes and being taken all over the ship by one of her jet pilots."

"Well, Your Highness, that Navy pilot is my husband and is sitting at the table right over there."

"This is marvelous," he said. "I can't wait to talk to him, but right now I'm being called to the podium to introduce Julie Andrews. Please tell your husband that we'll meet and talk after dinner."

Stefanie returned to our table and told me what happened and how excited the prince seemed to be in remembering his time with me on the carrier. Later on after dinner, our group joined many others on the spacious dance floor area. I saw John and Barbara as well as the prince and princess. After a while there was a break in the action, Stefanie and I walked over and began a conversation with the prince. I was thrilled to listen to his remembrances of his day with me—he seemed to remember details which I had forgotten.

"I have fond memories of that great day so long ago. Going all over the carrier with you, eating a meal with you and your pilot buddies were highlights. But watching the planes land on the flight deck was absolutely the greatest thrill."

Having been chosen to be the prince's personal escort during his and his father's, Prince Rainier, time aboard the *Sara*, I had taken the prince with me for several hours wherever I went—including to the LSO platform as I had the LSO duty that day.

I asked, "Your Highness, do you recall standing near me when I was doing my LSO duties and watching the tailhook grab a wire and bring the plane to a halt?"

"Of course, I remember watching the landings. That was the best part of my visit—it was very exciting and extremely noisy."

"While that was the best part for you, the most memorable part of your visit for me actually took place after you and your father left the ship," I told the prince. "I was called to the Air Boss's office where he read me the riot act for bringing you out to the platform. I don't know whether you remember but an F-4 Phantom II, had blown its port tire on touchdown during one of the recoveries and parts of the exploding rubber had flown very close to where we were standing. As the deck crew was clearing the debris from the landing area, the Boss saw you standing next to me. Needless to say, he seriously questioned my judgment and let me know that he disapproved of my decision to have you alongside me on the flight deck platform."

Prince Albert, Stefanie, and I had a good laugh over that story. He told us that he didn't recall any conversations with his father about that incident but was thankful that the only consequence to me was a tongue lashing by the Boss. Before he left us to join others socializing near the dance floor, the prince thanked us for coming to the event honoring his mother. He was so happy to meet me after all the years and be reminded of a most exciting and unforgettable experience from his childhood.

On our walk back to our hotel sometime later, Stef and I talked about the fabulous event and how wonderful it was to have friends like Mary Lou and Jim McCann and to be with Barbara and John Lehman and his second cousin, Prince Albert, His Serene Highness.

EPILOGUE

FOR MANY REASONS, I AM glad I waited to tell this story because earlier it wasn't as complete as it needed to be. Events happened to several of the key players which bear significantly on what Paul Harvey, for many years, use to call the "rest of the story":

2001

Most notable is that of Rear Adm. Wilson "Bud" Flagg, USNR (Ret.). He and his wife, Dee, had attended his Fortieth USNA Class Reunion in Annapolis the weekend of September 8–10, 2001. On Monday, September 11, they boarded an American Airlines flight from Dulles to LAX—their final destination was San Diego where they would see their new baby grandson. At 9:37 AM, their hijacked Boeing 757, Flt. 77, crashed into the Pentagon, killing all on board and 125 Pentagon personnel and injuring fifty-nine as well. Many were Navy personnel who were assigned to the Navy Command Center where I had once been a Navy Department duty captain from 1986 to 1989.

A week later, I was privileged to be at Bud and Dee's memorial service in the Naval Academy Chapel. Many hundreds of Bud's Navy and American Airlines friends attended this most sorrowful but beautiful event. Most appropriately, it was Adm. Dunleavy who delivered an inspiring and emotional eulogy.

(The day before, a memorial service at the Academy Chapel was held for Navy Capt. Charles Burlingame, USNR (Ret.), USNA Class of 1974. He had been the American Airlines captain of Flt. 77.)

2002

On July23, 2002 Assistant Secretary of the Navy (Manpower and Reserve Affairs), William Navas Jr., authorized the Board of Correction of Naval Records, to amend the personnel file of Cdr. Robert Stumpf, USN (Ret.) to show him retired as a captain, with the date of rank of July 1, 1995.

During the Gulf War, Stumpf had commanded an F/A-18 Squadron and subsequently became the leader of the Blue Angels but was suspended in that job in July 1993 by Vice Adm. Reason who was then in charge of the Tailhook investigations. He was cleared of any wrongdoing and was reassigned back to the Blues. A rising star in Naval Aviation, the Senate approved his promotion to captain in 1994 when he was slated to become commander of an air wing aboard the USS *Enterprise.* His promotion was subsequently pulled by SECNAV Dalton because his record had not been properly "flagged" to the Senate where his case became a source of intense debate among some very powerful Senators. After a series of investigations over a two-year period, Stumpf finally gave up his fight and retired in 1996. "When you summarily ruin the careers of a great many dedicated, patriotic, professional Navy officers for political reasons, you need to be held accountable" was a quote after he learned of his promotion.

2003

SECNAV Gordon England summoned Rear Adm. Riley Mixson, USN (Ret.) to his office and shortly thereafter convened a Board of Inquiry to examine former SECNAV Dalton's Letter of Censure of 1993. As a result of its recommendation, the letter was permanently removed from his official personnel file.

In conversations with Mark Flagg, Adm. Bud Flagg's son, I learned that the same type review by another Board of Inquiry would have been convened by SECNAV England if the Flagg family had requested it. Mark told me that the family declined to make the request since they believed that their deceased father thought that the letter was his own "red badge of courage" and would not have wanted it expunged from his record.

2008

Adm. Frank B Kelso II, USN (Ret.) was honored by the US Naval Academy Alumni Association as a "Distinguished Alumnus of the Year." Presented every year to a small number of alumni, his citation noted that "while planning for the future of the Navy, Adm. Kelso was jolted back to the present by the events of the Tailhook in 1991...(he) eliminated vestiges of an old and embedded culture to make way for a brighter future for all. Our core values of honor, commitment, and courage were initiated on his watch." (My letter to the chairman of the selection committee questioning Adm. Kelso's forced retirement went unanswered.)

2010

My wife, Stefanie, told me that several authors would probably be attending a "silent auction" summer fund-raiser in nearby Sag Harbor, and so I decided to attend as I was anxious to learn as much as I could about writing a nonfiction book. During a lull in the action, I was surveying the prizes on the tables when I spotted actor Richard Gere just feet away doing the same thing. I walked over to him and introduced myself and said, "Thank you, Mr. Gere, for doing a fantastic job in the film about my life." He said, "*An Officer and Gentleman*, no doubt you're a naval aviator." "Incredible," I said, "but how did you know?" He told me that we aviators are the only ones who have ever thanked him for acting out our stories. We had a short but delightful conversation in which he told me that several Marine drill instructors who acted in or advised on that movie remained as close friends. As we were separating, he asked if "I carried her [Debra Winger] off, too?" "No, not that time," was my answer.

2011

In doing research, I reread parts of John Lehman's book, *Command of the Seas*, and discovered that we shared an identical boyhood experience. While I had first heard the "whistling death" sound of the F-4U Corsairs in Sheepshead Bay and seen them at NAS Floyd Bennett, he had similarly gotten hooked watching and hearing them at NAS Willow Grove near Philadelphia. In our exchange of e-mails,

I pointed this out, and John suggested that "we should start a Corsair inspiration society, like the one made up of those conceived while their parents played Johnny Mathis records."

2012

I had known that Paula Coughlin Puopolo was the founder and director of Ocean Yoga Center located in Atlantic Beach, FL, for more than ten years. Since retirement from the navy in 1994, I'd occasionally read some news about her and a good part of the story always contained many of the same statements, such as "I was sexually assaulted by two hundred naval aviators"; "I blew the whistle on Tailhook"; "My admiral made light of and dismissed my claims"; "Sec. Cheney blamed me for having to fire the secretary of the Navy"; "President Bush cried when I told him what had happened." But in June 2012, I read a review in the *NY Times* about an award-winning film which had premiered at the Sundance Film festival in January titled *The Invisible War*. It was a documentary about rape and sexual assaults in the military, and Paula Puopolo played a part in it. Months later, I saw part of a press conference in DC where she spoke on behalf of *Protect Our Defenders*, a nonprofit organization which supports victims of sexual assault and rape in the Armed Forces. She is a member of its advocacy board.

Afterthoughts

In so many ways, Tailhook '91 was a watershed event that caused or helped to cause significant social and cultural changes in the Navy that were inevitable. Unfortunately, these changes were accompanied by personal and organizational tragedies of monumental proportions. I've attempted to highlight some officers, but there were many more whose stories are worth examining for what they tell us about the system in which the Navy operates. As was pointed out, some who were charged were cleared almost immediately. For others, the process took much longer. Even so, I'm reminded of President Reagan's secretary of labor, Ray Donovan, a golfing buddy, who was accused of fraud and resigned his Cabinet position. Two and one half years later, he was acquitted of all charges but asked a most important, though rhetorical, question, "Which office do I go to get my reputation back?"

Admirals Stanley Arthur and Jeremy Boorda, USN (Ret.) deserve critical books to be written about them because of the lessons we could learn. From my early Jesuit education in Brooklyn Prep, I was taught the necessity of always "doing the hard right, not the easy wrong." Both of these talented and gifted leaders faced this challenge and lived or died with the consequences.

Finally, I have given considerable thought to the question: "Could the devastating aftermath of Tailhook '91 been prevented?" Yes is the easy answer, but the follow-up question of "How?" is far more difficult to discern. Similar to catastrophic airplane accidents, Tailhook didn't happen because of one major action but rather a series of actions. Had any one in the sequence not happened, it's highly likely that the "crash" would not have occurred.

One of my favorite quotes, written by Sir Winston Churchill in *The Story of the Malakand Field Force*, is "Nothing in life is so exhilarating as to be shot at with no results." Those of us flyboys who have shared in this seminal experience during our stint in the military developed a special bond that unites all of us in ways that are strong and permanent. For that reason alone, I will always be most proud to call myself a Tailhooker and be a part of a very special "band of brothers."

ENDNOTES

1. Inspector General, DoD, Memorandum for the Acting Secretary of the Navy. Report of Investigation: Tailhook '91—Part 1, Report of Navy Investigations, September 21, 1992, PP 7-8, P 60
2. Captain F. G. Ludwig, Jr., The Tailhook Association letter, 11 October 1991. P 63
3. Captain Frederick G. Ludwig, Jr., The Tailhook Association letter, 15 August, 1991. P 63
4. H. Lawrence Garrett III, Secretary of the Navy Letter, 29 October 1991. P 64
5. H. Lawrence Garrett, III, Secretary of the Navy Memorandum for the Undersecretary of the Navy, 29 October 1991. P 64
6. Dan Howard, The Undersecretary of the Navy Memorandum for the Naval Inspector General, 29 October 1991. P 64
7. Thomas, Library of Congress, The Tailhook Association (Senate—October 29, 1991), http://thomas.loc.gov/cgi-bin/query/F?r102:25:./temp/~r102AvjF1T:e47:. P 65
8. *Frontline: The Navy Blues*: Interview with Sen. John McCain, PBS, http://www.pbs.org/wgbh/frontline/shows/navy/ails/mccain1.html. P 65
9. Howard, op. cit. P 72
10. J. E. Gordon, Rear Admiral, Judge Advocate General, Department of the Navy Memorandum for the Secretary of the Navy, 22 March 1992. P 76
11. H. Lawrence Garrett III, Secretary of the Navy Memorandum for the Chief of Naval Operations, Commandant of the Marine Corps, 2 June 1992. P 76

12. C-SPAN, http://www.c-span.org/video/?26420-1/manpower-issues-1993-defense-authorization. P 77
13. Robert Suro, "Panel Seeks to Resume Navy Promotions," *New York Times*, June 29, 1992. P 78
14. Eric Schmitt, "Navy Chief Quits Amid Questions over Role in Sex-Assault Inquiry," *The New York Times*, June 26, 1992. P 81
15. H. Lawrence Garrett III, statement, 11 June, 1992. P 81
16. Eric Schmitt, "Navy Chief Admits to Being Close By during Lewd Party," *New York Times*, June 16, 1992. P 86
17. Eric Schmitt, "Pentagon Takes Over Inquiry on Pilots," *New York Times*, June 18, 1992. P 87
18. John Lancaster, "A Gauntlet of Terror, Frustration-Navy Pilot Recounts Tailhook Incident," *Washington Post*, June, 24, 1992. P 88
19. Peter Jennings, "Nightly News, Transcripts of: Segment 1, June 24, 1992 and Segment 1, June 25, 1992," *ABC News*, June 24–25, 1992. P 89
20. Sam Donaldson, "Primetime: Transcript of June 26, 1992," *ABC News*, June 26, 1992. P 90
21. Neil A. Lewis, "President Meets Female Officer in Navy Incident," *New York Times*, June 27, 1992. P 90
22. Erin Solaro, *Women in the Line of Fire: What You Should Know about Women in the Military*, Seal Press, 2009, page 174. P 90
23. Eric Schmitt, June 26, 1992. P 91
24. Eric Schmitt, "Navy Chief Seeks Anti-Harassment Law," *New York Times*, July 2, 1992. P 89, P 92
25. John Lancaster, "Navy Orders Training on Harassment," *Washington Post*, July 3, 1992. P 93
26. H. G. Reza, "Five Officers at Miramar Are Relieved of Command," *Los Angeles Times*, July 25, 1992. P 94
27. H.G. Reza, "Navy Reinstates 2 Fliers Fired in Tomcat Follies," *Los Angeles Times*, August 15, 1992. P 94
28. John Lancaster, "Close Cheney Aide Appointed as Acting Secretary of the Navy," *Washington Post*, July 8, 1992. P 94

29. Sean O'Keefe, Acting Secretary of the Navy, Memorandum for the Chief of Naval Operations, Commandant of the Marine Corps, 9 July 1992. P 94
30. F. B. Kelso, Admiral, US Navy Chief of Naval Operations Memorandum for Commander in Chief, US Atlantic Fleet, Commander in Chief , US Pacific Fleet, Chief of Naval Education and Training, Chief of Navy Reserve, 10 July 1992. P 95
31. John Lancaster, "More to Get Ax in Navy Sex Scandal," *Washington Post*, September 24, 1992. P 95
32. John Lancaster, "Pentagon Blasts Tailhook Inquiry," *Washington Post*, September 25, 1992. P 95
33. Department of Defense, Office of the Inspector General, Report of Investigation: Tailhook '91—Part 1, Review of the Navy Investigations. 21 September 1992. P 95
34. Secretary Lawrence Garrett III, "Letter to Michael B. Suessman, Esq. Assistant Inspector General, DOD," August 25, 1992. P 96
35. Statement of Acting Secretary of the Navy Sean O'Keefe, "O'Keefe Responds to DoD IG Report," *Defense Issues,* Vol. 7 No. 50, September 24, 1992. P 96
36. Sean O'Keefe, Secretary of the Navy, Defense Department News Briefing, DoD IG Report, September 24, 1992, C-Span: http://www.c-span.org/video/?32720-1/defense-department-news-briefing. P 97
37. J. Robert Lunney, Captain, JAGC, USNR (Ret.), "Tailhook—The Other Side," *Naval Reserve Association News*, January, 1993, pp 7–21. P 99
38. J. Robert Lunney, Captain, JAGC, USNR (Ret.), "A Question of Fairness," *Naval Reserve Association News*, February, 1993, pp 7–11. P 99
39. Patrick Pexton, "Decision Delayed: Tailhook Cloud Still Hangs over Navy," *Navy Times*, March 8, 1993. P 104
40. Office of Assistant Secretary of Defense (Public Affairs), News Release, "Aspin Sends Tailhook Report to Navy," April 23, 1993. P 104

41. Frank B. Kelso, II, Admiral, Chief of Naval Operations, Statement on DoD IG Tailhook Report, April 23, 1993. P 104
42. Department of Defense, Office of the Inspector General, Report of Investigation: Tailhook '91—Part 2, Events of the 35th Annual Tailhook Symposium, April 12, 1993. P 105
43. John Lancaster, "Tailhook Probe Implicates 140 Officers," *Washington Post*, April 24, 1993. P 107
44. Maureen Dowd, "Testimony Conflicts at Military Hearings on Abuse by Fliers," *New York Times*, August 18, 1883. P 111
45. Neil A. Lewis. "Officer Cleared in Main Tailhook Case," *New York Times*, October 22, 1993. P 112
46. Stansfield Turner, "Letting the Big Fish Off the Tailhook Hook," *Washington Post*, January 24, 1993. P 134
47. John H. Dalton, Secretary of the Navy Statement Regarding the Status of 35 Flag and General Officers, *US Navy Press Release*, October 15, 1993. P 135
48. Donna Cassata, "Admiral Punished in Tailhook Scandal Says He Is a 'Scapegoat,'" *Associated Press*, October 29. 1993. P 135
49. Wilson F. Flagg, Rear Admiral, USNR, Rebuttal to Letter of Censure, 26 October 1993. P 136
50. Jim Starling, "Kelso, Garrett, Dunleavy Take Stand in Tailhook," *Soundings*, Vol. 19, No. 48, December 1, 1993. P 140
51. Kerry DeRochi, "Reservist: Kelso Heard Fliers Urge Women to Strip," *Virginian-Pilot*, Dec.14, 1992. P 146
52. Eric Schmitt, "Military Court Assails Navy in Ruling on Tailhook," *New York Times*, January 12, 1994. P 153
53. General Court-Martial, United States Navy, Tidewater Judicial Court, Norfolk, Virginia: United States v. Thomas R Miller; Gregory E. Tritt; David Samples, February 7, 1994. P 154
54. See: Eric Schmitt, "Judge Dismisses Tailhook Cases, Saying Admiral Tainted Inquiry," *New York Times*, February 9, 1994.
    Andrea Stone, "Court: Tailhook Cover-Up Tried," *USA Today*, February 9, 1994.
    Rowan Scarborough, "Navy Judge Says Kelso Lied in Tailhook Probe," *Washington Times*, February 9, 1994. P 155

55. Times Wire Services, "Last Charges Are Dropped by Navy in Tailhook Probe," *Los Angeles Times*, February 12, 1994. P 156
56. Tim Weiner, "The Navy Decides Not to Appeal Dismissals of Last Tailhook Cases," *New York Times*, February 12, 1994. P 156
57. Weiner, February 12, 1994. P 156
58. Eric Schmitt' "In Tailhook Deal, Top Admiral Says He'll Retire Early," *New York Times*, February 16, 1994. P 157
59. New York Times News Service, "Aspin Rejects Navy Secretary's Advice, Won't Fire Top Admiral over Tailhook," *The Baltimore Sun*, October 6, 1993. P 157
60. Michael Ross and Karen Tumulty, "Senate to Retire Kelso at 4 Stars, After Fiery Debate," *Los Angeles Times,* April 20, 1994. See also: Maureen Dowd, "Senate Approves a 4-Star Rank for Admiral in Tailhook Affair," *The New York Times*, April 19, 1994. P 158
61. Times Wire Services, op. cit. P 159
62. Bernard Ryan, Jr., "Paula Coughlin v. The Las Vegas Hilton: 1994," http://law.jrank.org/pages/3615/Paula-Coughlin-v-Las-Vegas-Hilton-1994-Coughlin-Sues-Hilton.html. P 159

APPENDIX A

Chronology

August 15, 1991 – Capt. Ludwig sends pre-Tailhook letter to squadron Tailhook representatives.

September 5–8, 1991 – 35th Annual Tailhook Symposium at the Las Vegas Hilton

September 8, 1991 – Rear Adm. Snyder and staff including Lieutenant Paula Coughlin meet for breakfast

September 19, 1991 – Rear Adm. Snyder and Lieutenant Paula Coughlin meet at the admiral's office at NAS Patuxent River.

September 29, 1991 – Rear Adm. Snyder delivers his and Lieutenant Coughlin's letters to Vice Adm. Dunleavy who delivers them to the VCNO, Adm. Jerome Johnson

October 11, 1991 – The NIS begins a criminal investigation of Tailhook at the direction of the VCNO.

October 11, 1991 – Capt. Ludwig sends his debrief letter to all squadron commanding officers.

October 29, 1991 – Secretary of the Navy H. Lawrence Garrett III sends letter to Capt. Ludwig admonishing him for the conduct at Tailhook and severing all Navy relationships with the Tailhook Association.

October 29, 1991 – Sen. McCain condemns Tailhook on the Senate floor after meeting with Lieutenant Coughlin.

October 29, 1991 – Sec. Garrett directs the undersecretary to task the Navy IG to conduct a noncriminal investigation of Tailhook.

November 4, 1991 – The CNO temporarily relieves Adm. Snyder of his command.

December 20, 1991 – CNO permanently relieves Adm. Snyder of his command.

April 30, 1992 – Undersecretary Howard releases the NIS and IG reports.

June 18, 1992 – Sec. Garrett asks the DoD IG to investigate the Navy's investigations of Tailhook '91.

June 24–25, 1992 – Lieutenant Coughlin gives press interviews and is on ABC's *World News Tonight* with Peter Jennings.

June 26, 1992 – Lieutenant Paula Coughlin meets with the President and Mrs. George H. W. Bush at the White House.

June 26, 1992 – Sec. Garrett resigns. Undersecretary Howard is appointed acting secretary.

July 7, 1992 – Sean O'Keefe named acting secretary of the Navy by SECDEF Cheney.

September 24, 1992 – DoD IG issues Part 1 of its report.

September 24, 1992 – Sec. O'Keefe announces retirement of Rear Admirals Williams and Gordon and reassignment of Rear Adm. Davis.

January 23, 1993 – SECDEF Aspin takes over DoD and Adm. Kelso is named acting SECNAV.

January 26, 1993 – Vice Adm. J. Paul Reason and Lt. Gen. Charles Krulak chosen by Adm. Kelso to be the CDA's for the Navy and Marine Corps, respectfully.

February 1993 – SECDEF Aspin receives DoD IG Report Part 2.

April 21, 1993 – John H. Dalton is nominated to be secretary of the Navy.

April 23, 1993 – Navy releases DoD IG Report Part 2.

July 22, 1993 – John Dalton becomes the secretary of the Navy and is given the files of flag and general officers.

October 15, 1993 – Sec. Dalton gives three admirals—Dunleavy, Mixson, and Flagg "letters of censure." He gives thirty admirals and generals "non-punitive letters of caution."

November 8, 1993 – Commander Miller's court-martial begins.

November, 29, 1993 – CNO Adm. Kelso and Vice Adm. Dunleavy testify in Capt. Vest's Norfolk court room at the courts-martial of Commanders Miller and Tritt.

December 13, 1993 – The author testifies in Capt. Vest's courtroom.

December 17, 1993 – Capt. Vest declares the court-martial now in recess. He will issue his ruling in several weeks.

February 8, 1994 – Capt. Vest issues ruling: Charges against Commanders Miller, Tritt, and Lieutenant Samples are dismissed without prejudice.

February 10, 1994 – Vice Adm. Reason announces no further prosecutions of Tailhook offenders.

February 15, 1994 – CNO Adm. Frank Kelso announces his early retirement.

April 19, 1994 – Senate approves Adm. Kelso's retirement at four-star level.

April 23, 1994 – Adm. Jeremy Boorda relieves Adm. Frank Kelso as CNO at a ceremony at the US Naval Academy.

May 31, 1994 – Lieutenant Paula Coughlin is released from active duty.

September 8, 1994 – Lieutenant Coughlin and Tailhook reach a pre-trial settlement.

September 12, 1994 – Court trial of Lt. Paula Coughlin v. Hilton Hotels and Las Vegas Hilton begins.

October 1, 1994 – Author retires as a captain from the US Naval Reserve.

May 2, 1997 – $5.2 million award to Paula Coughlin upheld by appellate court.

APPENDIX B

THE TAILHOOK ASSOCIATION
P.O. Box 40
Bonita, CA 91908-0040

Phone: (619) 689-9223

15 August 1991

NFWS
NAS MIRAMAR
SAN DIEGO, CA 92145

Dear Tailhook Representative:

Enclosed you will find a copy of the floor plan and the location of your suite. If you have any questions, please feel free to contact Tailhook at our toll free number 1-800-322-HOOK. Please be patient, our lines are crazy this time of year.

This year we want to make sure everyone is aware of certain problems we've had in past year's.

As last year, you will only be charged for damage inside your suite. The Association will pay for common area damage. In order to keep damage charges to a minimum inside your suite, please make sure you check-in with someone from the Association. You may do this by calling the Tailhook Suite prior to moving into your suite. Our representative, a Hilton representative from housekeeping, and you will go over your suite prior to move-in. Please make sure you sign the form our representative will have and retain a copy. On Sunday, 9 September we will again inspect the suites in the same manner. Damage not listed on the check-in form will be the squadron's responsibility. If you do not check-in with the Association we will not be able to dispute any damage charges made by the Hilton Hotel.

In past years we have had a problem with under age participants. If you see someone who does not look like they belong in our group, or look under age please ask for a ID. If they are under age, or do not have ID, please ask them to leave or contact Security. It is important that we try to eliminate those under the age of 21. If they were to leave the hotel and cause an accident, hurting themselves or anyone else, the Association, along with the squadron, the Navy, and the Hilton could be sued and Tailhook would come to an end. Please assist us in this matter.

Also, in the past we have had a problem with late night "gang mentality." If you see this type of behavior going on, please make an effort to curtail it either by saying something, calling security or contacting someone from the Association. We will have people on the floor in blue committee shirts should you need them for any reason.

Tailhook will also have a flight surgeon aboard this year. Should you, or anyone you know need a "DOC", please call the Tailhook Suite or make contact with a committee member. Security will also have his beeper number.

Remember, when bringing in your suite supplies do so with discretion. We are not allowed to bring certain articles into the Hilton. Please cover your supplies by putting them in parachute bags or boxes. DO NOT BORROW LAUNDRY BASKETS FROM THE

. . . to foster, encourage, study, develop and support the aircraft carrier, sea-based aircraft, both fixed and rotary wing, and aircrew . . .

C000336

HILTON. THEIR SENSE OF HUMOR DOES NOT GO THAT FAR!!!

Supplies may be purchased in town from "WOW". They have a number of items that may be purchased or rented for your suite. The lanai suites do not have wet bars. You will need to set-up your own bar. The Hilton does not supply such items.

We suggest you remove your telephones from your suite so you are not paying for someone elses long distance calls. This has happened in the past. Also, make sure the phones are returned to the room. This is an item we have all forgotten to check on our check-in/check-out inspection. Please look for outlets in your suite by the beds and in the bathroom. Almost all suites have a phone outlet in the bathroom. It IS VERY IMPORTANT THAT YOU CHECK THE BATHROOM FOR A PHONE OR AN OUTLET and note it!

Please make sure your duty officers are SOBER and prepared to handle any problems that may arise in your suite. It is necessary for them to be willing to work with the Association staff. We will make every effort to handle all problems.

REMEMBER....THERE ARE TO BE NO "QUICK HIT" DRINKS served. LEWD AND LASCIVIOUS behavior is unacceptable. The behavior in your suite reflects on both your squadron and your commanding officer.

Have a great time. Thank you for your continued support of the Tailhook Association. We look forward to seeing you in Las Vegas.

Sincerely,

Frederic G. Ludwig, Jr.
Captain, U. S. Navy
President

APPENDIX C

THE TAILHOOK ASSOCIATION

PRESIDENT
CAPT Frederic G. Ludwig, Jr. USN

VICE PRESIDENTS

Industrial Affairs
G. C. "Buddy" Gilman

Corporate Development CDR
Howard E. Ruggles, USN(Ret)

Reserve Affairs
LCDR William McKinnon USNR

Marine Affairs
COL M. A. Rietsch, USMC

Educational Activity
LCDR David W. Colly USN

BOARD OF DIRECTORS

Chairman Emeritus
CAPT F. A. W. Franke, Jr. USN(Ret)

Chairman
CAPT W. D. "Bill" Knutson, USN(Ret) CAPT R. F. "Skip" Braden USN
CAPT Michael J. McCabe USN
CAPT "Cal" Swanson, USN(Ret)
CAPT Wynn F. Foster, USN(Ret)
CAPT Terry E. Magee, USN LCOL C. L. "Chuck" Zangas, USMC(Ret)
LCDR James P. Usbeck, USN

Advisor, Naval Aviation Matters
RADM James D. Ramage, USN(Ret)

Executive Director
Ron Thomas

General Counsel
J. Wesley Fry

Treasurer
CAPT "Cal" Swanson, USN(Ret)

EDITOR
CAPT Stephen T. Millikin USN(Ret)

MANAGING EDITOR
Jan C. Jacobs

ASSOCIATE EDITORS
CAPT Wynn F. Foster USN(Ret)
Barrett Tillman
CWO4 Carl W. Snow USN(Ret)

CARRIER EDITOR
Robert J. Cressman

EDITORIAL COMMITTEE
RADM James D. Ramage USN(Ret)

CONTRIBUTING EDITORS
CDR Doug Siegfried, USN(Ret)
CDR Pete Clayton, USN Hal Andrews

CONTRIBUTING PHOTOGRAPHERS
Douglas D. Olson
Michael E. Grove
Bruce R. Trombecky
Keith Snyder

Information regarding Tailhook Symposiums is available from the Tailhook Association. Editorial matters only are handled at The Hook address.

Articles and news items are welcomed. Submit material for THE HOOK to

Editorial Offices The Hook

TAILHOOK '91 AGENDA

THURSDAY, 5 SEPTEMBER 1991

0900 READY ROOM AND EXHIBITS OPEN. . . . . BARRON ROOM
ALL SYMPOSIUM PROGRAMS WILL BE HELD IN PAVILLION AREA
1600-1630 TAILHOOK ASSOCIATION MEETING
1630-1700 AVIATION SAFETY . . . RADM J. B. FINNEY (COMNAVSAFECEN)
1700-1730 ADVANCE AIRCRAFT TECHNOLOGIES . . . MR. T. MORGENFELD (LOCKHEAD NAFT TEST PILOT)
1800 EXHIBITS CLOSED
1900-2100 NO HOST COCKTAIL PARTY/EXHIBITS OPEN . . . BARRON ROOM
2100 REGISTRATION BOOTH CLOSED

FRIDAY, 6 SEPTEMBER 1991

0730 GOLF AND TENNIS TOURNAMENTS
0900 REGISTRATION AND EXHIBITS OPEN. . . . . BARRON ROOM
ALL SYMPOSIUM PROGRAMS WILL BE HELD IN PAVILLION AREA
1030-1045 SYMPOSIUM INTRODUCTION . . . VADM R. M. DUNLEAVY (OP-05)
CAPT F. G. LUDWIG (TAILHOOK PRESIDENT)
1045-1245 DESERT STORM NAVAL OPERATIONS

-MASTER COORDINATED STRIKE PLAN. . . . . CAPT L. G. BIEN
-PERSIAN GULF... CAPT J. BURIN (CVW-5)
-RED SEA . . . . CAPT W. J. FALLON (CVW-8)
-BAHRAIN/SAUDI ARABIA..... . .COL D. BEAUFAIT (MAG-11)

1245-1300 HOOKER HOTDOGS

APPENDIX C

1300-1400 NAVAL AIR SYSTEMS DESERT STORM
MUNITIONS EFFECTIVENESS BRIEFINGS

- TOMAHAWK' . . . . LCDR B. JOHANSON (STRIKE U)
-AIR-GROUND PROGRAMS . CAPT B. RAMSAY (PMA-201)
-AIR-AIR PROGRAMS . . CDR T. MCKENZIE (OP-501)

1400-11515 DESERT STORM RECONNAISSANCE/ SURVEILLANCE/INTELLIGENCE OVERVIEW

- INTEL/JOINT STARS. . . . . . . CAPT. C. JOHNSON (SPEARS)
- TARPS.............................LDCR D. PARSONS (VF-32)/LT P. MONGER (VF-2)
-RPVs...........CAPT A. C. AUER (3rd RPV CO)

1515-1545 MIG KILLER DEBRIEF. . . . . . LT N. MONGELLO (VFA-81)

1545-1630 PRISONER OF WAR EXPERIENCES. . . . . CAPT C. BERRYMAN
LT R. SLADE
LT R. WETZEL

1630-1700 DESERT STORM STRIKE RESCUE OPERATIONS. . . . . CDR M. MCCARTY (OP-503F)
MR. R. MASTRONARDI (SIKORSKY AIRCRAFT)

1700-1730 F-18 E/F...............CAPT C. STRIDLE (PFA-265)

1730-1800 AX: NAVAL STRIKE FIGHTER. . . . . RADM J. TAYLOR (OP-05)

1800-1830 RESERVE OFFICER MEETING. . . . . RADM R. K. CHAMBERS (COMNAVAIRESFOR)

1800 EXHIBITS CLOSED

1900-2100 COCKTAIL PARTY AND BUFFET (NO HOST AFTER 2000) .... BARRON ROOM

SATURDAY, 7 SEPTEMBER 1991

0700 5K FUN RUN
0900 EXHIBITS OPEN. . . . . BARRON ROOM
0900-0930 AVIATION PERSONNEL ISSUES . . . . . . RADM J. L. JOHNSON (BUPERS)
0930-1000 CARRIER PLANSINAVAL AIR STATION PLANS. . . . . RADM R. P. HICKEY (OP-05)
1000-1030 CARRIER AIR WING PLANS . . . . RADM R. D. MIXSON (OP-05B)
1030-1100 NAVAL AVIATION BUDGET OVERVIEW. . . . . RADM J. TAYLOR (OP-50)
1100-1200 STATE OF NAVAL AVIATION ADDRESS. . . . . VADM R. M. DUNLEAVY (OP-05)
1200-1400 AWARDS LUNCH-PAVILLION
1400-1405 FIGHTS ON, FIGHTS ON IV ..., ... CUBIC CORP
1405-1420 ASSOCIATION OF NAVAL AVIATION. . . . . VADM W. P. LAWRENCE
1420-1435 TAILHOOK ASSOCIATION BUILDING FUND UPDATE. . . . . CAPT W. KNUTSON
1435 FLAG PANEL. . . VADM R. M. DUNLEAVY (OP-05)
VADM J. B. FETTERMAN, JR. (CNET)
VADM E. R. KOHN (CNAP)
VADM A. A. LESS (CNAL)
LGEN D. A. WILLS (HQMC)
VADM W. C. BOWES (CNASC)
RADM R. K. CHAMBERS (CNARF)
RADM W. R. MCGOWEN (CNATRA)
RADM J. L. JOHNSON (BUPERS)
CAPT F. G. LUDWIG (MODERATOR)
1500-1800 EXHIBITS CLOSED'
1800 NO HOST COCKTAIL PARTY /EXHIBITS OPEN.......................................BARRON ROOM
1900 BANQUET-PAVILLION ....HONORABLE
H. LAWRENCE GARRETT, III,
SECRETARY OF THE NAVY

SUNDAY, 8 SEPTEMBER 1991

AM BUFFET BRUNCH-PAVILLION
1200 CHECK OUT

APPENDIX D

THE TAILHOOK ASSOCIATION
P.O. Box 40
Bonita, CA 91908-0040

Phone: (619) 689-9223

11 October 1991

Dear Skipper,

As President of the Tailhook Association, I wanted to take this opportunity to give you a debrief of the "goods" and "others" of this year's annual symposium at the Las Vegas Hilton while it is still fresh in your mind. Without a doubt, this was the biggest and most successful Tailhook we have ever had. We said it would be the "Mother of all Hooks", and it was. We had close to 5,000 people in attendance, over 1,500 rooms filled and 172 exhibits. The professional symposium proceeded flawlessly and it appeared the information exchange was excellent. The flag panel was a resounding success with an estimated 2,500 in attendance. The questions were frank, on the mark and often quite animated. Our banquet and luncheon also boasted of incredible attendance and were enjoyed by all. Our very senior naval leadership, including the Secretary and the CNO, were thoroughly impressed and immensely enjoyed their time at Tailhook '91. Additionally, all of our naval aviation leaders and many industry leaders had nothing but praise for the event. We can be proud of a tremendous Tailhook '91 and a great deal of thanks goes to all the young JOs in the various committees that made Hook fly.

But Tailhook '91 was the "Mother of all Hooks" in one other way, and that brings me to the "others." The major "other" of this year's symposium comes under the title of "unprofessionalism," and I mean unprofessionalism underlined! Let me relate just a few specifics to show how far across the line of responsible behavior we went.

This year our total damage bill was to the tune of $23,000.00. Of that figure, $18,000 was to install new carpeting as a result of cigarette burns and drink stains. We narrowly avoided a disaster when a "pressed ham" pushed out an eighth-floor window which subsequently fell on the crowd below. Finally, and definitely the most serious, was "the Gauntlet" on the third floor. I have five separate reports of young ladies, several of whom had nothing to do with Tailhook, who were verbally abused, had drinks thrown on them, were physically abused and were sexually molested. Most distressing was the fact an underage young lady was severely intoxicated and had her clothing removed by members of the Gauntlet.

C001339

I don't have to tell you that this type of behavior has put a very serious blemish on what was otherwise a successful symposium. It has further given a black eye to the Tailhook Association and all of Naval Aviation. Our ability to conduct future Tailhooks has been put at great risk due to the rampant unprofessionalism of a few. Tailhook cannot and will not condone the blatant and total disregard of individual rights and public/private property!

I, as your president, will do damage control work at regaining our rapport with the Las Vegas Hilton and attempt to lock-in Tailhook '92. I need you to get these "goods" and "others" briefed to all those who where in attendance under your purview. Further, I need you, as the leaders of our hardcharging JOs, to make them realize that if future Tailhooks are to take place, attitudes and behavior must change. We in Naval Aviation and the Tailhook Association are bigger and better than this.

As we plan for next year's Hook, I look forward to hearing from you on any ideas you might have to help eliminate unprofessional behavior during Tailhook '92. The intent is not in any way to keep from having fun. Rather, we have to figure out a way to have a great time responsibly, or we will jeopardize the very future of Tailhook altogether.

Warm Regards,

F. G. Ludwig, Jr.

F. G. LUDWIG, JR.
Captain USN
President, Tailhook Association

C001?40

APPENDIX E

THE SECRETARY OF THE NAVY
WASHINGTON, D. C. 20350-1000

29 October 1991

Captain F. G. Ludwig, Jr.
President
Tailhook Association
Post Office Box 40
Bonita, California 91906-0040

Dear Captain Ludwig,

I am writing to you, and through you to your organization, to express my absolute outrage over the conduct reported to have taken place at the Tailhook Association symposium in September as expressed in your letter of 11 October, a copy of which was provided me yesterday.

Besides my anger, I am more than personally disappointed. The Tailhook Association has been, in the past, a source of great professionalism and esprit, an organization where productive dialogues and seminars have had a home. In particular, Tailhook '91 provided me with a superb forum to air some of the most serious issues that Naval Aviation has ever faced. But none of those attributes can make up for the personal abuses, behavioral excesses, and quite possibly criminal conduct that took place at Tailhook '91 and have now been reported to me.

There are certain categories of behavior and attitudes that I unequivocally will not tolerate. You know the phrase: "Not in my Navy, not on my watch." Tailhook '91 is a gross example of exactly what cannot be permitted by the civilian or uniformed leadership of the Navy, at any level. No man who holds a commission in this Navy will ever subject a woman to the kind of abuse in evidence at Tailhook '91 with impunity. And no organization which makes possible this behavior is in any way worthy of a naval leadership or advisory role.

Admiral Frank Kelso, our Chief of Naval Operations, and I have discussed this matter and, based upon his recommendation and with his full support, I am terminating, effective immediately, all Navy support in any manner whatsoever, direct or indirect, for the Tailhook Association.

Last April I sent a message to every command in the Navy about the progress of our women officers and sailors. I said then that I would reinforce a position of zero tolerance of sexual harassment, and I meant it. That policy was not new in April, nor when I became Secretary--but obviously it was as necessary then as it is now to reiterate just how strongly I feel about this matter. Also in April, with my strong concurrence,

Admiral Kelso made specifically clear in a parallel message that a Navy free from sexual harassment or intimidation is a leadership issue. Together we made certain that the whole Navy knew: "Each of you, from the most junior sailor to the most senior officer, has a responsibility to build working and living spaces free from unprofessional conduct, fear, and prejudice." The Tailhook Association most certainly did not live up to that responsibility.

Very truly yours,

H. Lawrence Garrett, III
Secretary of the Navy

APPENDIX F

THE SECRETARY OF THE NAVY
WASHINGTON, D. C. 20350

29 OCT 91

MEMORANDUM FOR THE UNDER SECRETARY OF THE NAVY

Subj: Circumstances Surrounding the 35th Annual Tailhook Symposium

Please task the Inspector General of the Navy immediately to conduct a thorough investigation of any non-criminal abuses or violations of law or regulation that may be associated with the Tailhook Association, or subject Symposium.

H. Lawrence Garrett, III
Secretary of the Navy

APPENDIX G

THE UNDER SECRETARY OF THE NAVY
WASHINGTON, DC 20350-1000

29 OCT 91

MEMORANDUM FOR THE NAVAL INSPECTOR GENERAL

Subj: 35th ANNUAL TAILHOOK SYMPOSIUM

1. You are directed to conduct an investigation into organization and support of the Tailhook Association, as well as the conduct of subject symposium, including, but not limited to, the following issues:

- the propriety of utilization of naval resources, including military aircraft, vehicles and official travel funds in support of subject symposium,

- the nature, extent, and propriety of the relationship of the Tailhook Association and the Navy,

- the professional climate associated with subject symposium, to include adherence to Department of the Navy policy concerning consumption of alcohol and sexual abuse,

- any other administrative or regulatory abuses or violations that may have occurred.

2. Any evidence of criminal misconduct shall be referred to Commander, Naval Investigative Service, for appropriate action.

3. I request your completion of this investigation not later than 30 days from receipt of this memorandum. Please provide me interim reports on a weekly basis.

Dan Howard
Under Secretary of the Navy

APPENDIX H

DEPARTMENT OF THE NAVY
OFFICE OF THE SECRETARY
WASHINGTON, D.C. 20350

9 July 1992

MEMORANDUM FOR THE CHIEF OF NAVAL OPERATIONS
COMMANDANT OF THE MARINE CORPS

Subj: TAILHOOK '91

As explained in Secretary Garrett's memo to you of 25 June 1992, the Inspector General of the Department of Defense (DoD IG), requested further proceedings to investigate or to take administrative or disciplinary action on any matters related to Tailhook '91 be deferred until otherwise notified. Please ensure that request has been implemented and report back to me.

The DoD IG is conducting further inquiry into the events surrounding the 1991 Tailhook convention and reviewing the Navy investigations that followed. I expect full cooperation with this effort by all uniformed members and civilian employees of the Department of the Navy. Please ensure that the DoD IG is provided unrestricted access to all records, files, and other data considered relevant to the inquiry. In particular, every effort should be made on an individual basis to cooperate fully with the DoD IG's oral interviews into this matter.

Finally, I believe it is necessary for you to remind all personnel that the DoD IG Hotline number is 1-800-424-9098. Anyone with information relevant to the DoD IG investigation should be encouraged to call.

Sean O'Keefe
Secretary of the Navy
Acting

APPENDIX I

DEPARTMENT OF THE NAVY
OFFICE OF THE CHIEF OF NAVAL OPERATIONS
WASHINGTON, DC 20350-2000

IN REPLY REFER TO
Ser 00/2U500175
10 July 1992

MEMORANDUM FOR COMMANDER IN CHIEF, U.S. ATLANTIC FLEET
COMMANDER IN CHIEF, U.S. PACIFIC FLEET
CHIEF OF NAVAL EDUCATION AND TRAINING
CHIEF OF NAVAL RESERVE

Subj: TAILHOOK '91

Encl: (1) SECNAV memo dtd 9 July 1992

1. At the request of the Secretary of the Navy and with my full concurrence, the Inspector General of the Department of Defense (DoD IG) agreed on 24 June to conduct a further inquiry into the events that transpired at the 1991 Tailhook convention and to review the Navy investigations that followed. The DoD IG requested that disciplinary actions or further inquiries related to Tailhook '91 be held in abeyance until otherwise notified. Please ensure that request has been implemented and report back to me.

2. Mr. O'Keefe and I expect full cooperation with this effort. It is crucial to the future of the Navy and naval aviation that all hands rid our service of the blemish caused by this incident and its aftermath. Only by straightforwardly addressing the misconduct that occurred will the reputation of individuals and this institution be restored. As specified in enclosure (1), you should ensure that the DoD IG is provided unrestricted access to all records, files, and other data considered relevant to the inquiry. In particular, every effort should be made on an individual basis to cooperate fully with the DoD IG's oral interviews into the matter.

3. All personnel should be made aware that the DoD IG Hotline number is 1-800-424-9098. Anyone with information relevant to the DoD IG investigation is encouraged to call.

4. I know I can count on your honor, your integrity and your sense of duty.

F. B. Kelso II

F. B. KELSO II
Admiral, U.S. Navy
Chief of Naval Operations

Copy to:
OP-09
OP-01
NAVINSGEN
COMNISCOM
JAG

APPENDIX J

DEPARTMENT OF DEFENSE
400 ARMY NAVY DRIVE
ARLINGTON, VIRGINIA 22202-2884

SEP 21 1992

MEMORANDUM FOR ACTING SECRETARY OF THE NAVY

SUBJECT: Report of Investigation: Tailhook 91 - Part 1, Review of the Navy Investigations

We have completed the first of two reports regarding Tailhook 91. The enclosed report, "Tailhook 91 - Part 1, Review of the Navy Investigations," addresses the actions of senior Navy officials, the Naval Investigative Service (NIS) and the Naval Inspector General (Naval IG) in conducting earlier probes into Tailhook 91.

In part, we concluded that the scope of the investigations should have been expanded beyond the assaults to encompass other violations of law and regulation as they became apparent and should have addressed individual accountability for the leadership failure that created an atmosphere in which the assaults and other misconduct took place. We also concluded that the inadequacies in the investigations were due to the collective management failures and personal failures on the part of the Under Secretary, the Navy IG, the Navy JAG and the Commander of the NIS. In our view, the deficiencies in the investigations were the result of an attempt to limit the exposure of the Navy and senior Navy officials to criticism regarding Tailhook 91.

For reasons apart from our findings, I believe that changes may be warranted in the naval investigative structure. Since we cannot demonstrate that any particular change would have prevented the problems detailed in the enclosed report or that such changes would preclude similar errors in the future, I plan to discuss this aspect with you after you have had an opportunity to review the report.

We are continuing our investigation into the events that occurred at Tailhook 91 and will provide you the results at its conclusion.

Your response within 30 days will be appreciated. Should you have any questions, please contact me or Mr. Michael B. Suessmann, Assistant Inspector General for Departmental Inquiries, at (703) 697-6582.

Derek J. Vander Schaaf
Deputy Inspector General

APPENDIX K

INSPECTOR GENERAL
DEPARTMENT OF DEFENSE
400 ARMY NAVY DRIVE
ARLINGTON, VIRGINIA 22202-2884

April 12, 1993

MEMORANDUM FOR SECRETARY OF DEFENSE

SUBJECT: Report of Investigation: Tailhook 91 - Part 2, Events of the 35th Annual Tailhook Symposium

We have completed the second of two reports regarding Tailhook 91. The enclosed report, "Tailhook 91 - Part 2, Events at the 35th Annual Tailhook Symposium," describes what transpired at the Las Vegas Hilton Hotel between September 8 and 12, 1991. The report, which was completed in mid-February, provides information on the status of our investigation as of January 31, 1993.

Misconduct at the 1991 Tailhook Symposium was more widespread than previously reported by the Navy. We identified 90 victims of indecent assault. In addition, we documented a significant number of incidents of indecent exposure, and other types of sexual misconduct, as well as other improprieties by Navy and Marine Corps officers. We established that more than 50 officers made false statements to us during the investigation.

Investigative files on at least 140 officers are being referred to the Acting Secretary of the Navy for consideration of appropriate action. All individual files and records developed during the investigation will be made available to the convening authorities for review. Administrative or disciplinary action may be warranted against other officers whose actions and conduct are described in these records.

In addition, investigative files regarding the 30 Navy flag officers, 2 Marine Corps general officers and 3 Navy Reserve flag officers who attended Tailhook 91 will be forwarded to the Acting Secretary of the Navy after you have had an opportunity to review them. I believe the files pertaining to the flag officers should be evaluated outside of the convening authorities to determine whether action is warranted with respect to the responsibility of each flag officer for the overall leadership failure that culminated in the events of Tailhook 91.

I would appreciate being advised of the actions taken by you or the Navy with respect to the report. I will, of course, make myself and the OIG staff available to discuss the matter further with the new Secretary of the Navy, the Chief of Naval Operations, the Commandant of the Marine Corps, the convening authorities and their legal staffs.

Derek J. Vander Schaaf
Deputy Inspector General

Enclosure

APPENDIX L

No. 173-93
(703) 695-0192 (media)
(703) 697-3189 (copies)
(703) 697-5737 (public/industry)

IMMEDIATE RELEASE April 23, 1993

ASPIN SENDS TAILHOOK REPORT TO NAVY

Defense Secretary Les Aspin today transmitted to the Navy the second and final installment of the report from the Defense Department Inspector General's office on the Tailhook '91 naval aviator's convention that investigators say was marked by sexual harassment and indecent assault.

"I expect fair, thorough and impartial action on the cases and issues raised by this most regrettable episode, and will accept nothing less," Aspin said.

In addition to passing the report to the Navy, Aspin said he would direct Defense Department personnel officials to examine the report to determine if any changes should be made in policies and practices at the Defense Department level to help prevent sexual abuse and harassment in the Armed Forces.

"I make no judgment about individual cases arising from Tailhook. Appropriate procedures are in place to make those judgments and those procedures must be scrupulously fair and impartial. But I also serve notice that the kind of behavior reported by the Deputy Inspector General to have taken place will not be tolerated," Aspin said.

Aspin had earlier said he was holding the report until a new Navy Secretary was nominated and confirmed. The intention to nominate John H. Dalton to be Secretary of the Navy has been announced by the White House.

"We have every hope that the Senate will confirm Mr. Dalton. In the meantime, he can keep himself informed about Tailhook issues. Any action required by the Navy Secretary will come later in the process. By the time review by senior civilian leadership would become necessary, Mr. Dalton should be confirmed," Aspin said.

(more)

APPENDIX L

"The approach we are taking does four important things. First, it permits civilian oversight of the process, which was my goal from the start. Second, it starts to deal with those responsible. Third, it begins to remove the cloud of Tailhook that has shadowed the careers of many Navy and Marine officers who were not involved. Finally, it avoids the perception that senior uniformed leadership is the sole judge of its own behavior," the secretary said.

Deputy Inspector General Derek J. Vander Schaaf presented the results of his investigation of Tailhook '91 in two ways. The first comprised investigative files on cases in which Vander Schaaf believes sexual misconduct or other improper activity by individuals may have occurred. These files were conveyed to Navy by the deputy inspector general, but not made public.

The Navy and Marine Corps have identified a vice admiral and a lieutenant general, respectively, with no prior involvement in Tailhook matters to serve as the authorities to evaluate these investigative files.

"By the time these cases could be ready for high-level civilian review, John Dalton and other civilian Navy officials should be in place," Aspin said.

The second category of information from Vander Schaaf comprised files of officers who attended Tailhook and, by virtue of their positions and rank, may have to shoulder some responsibility for conduct at Tailhook.

In a memorandum to Aspin, Vander Schaaf said the existence of these files "should not be interpreted as an indication of any impropriety or neglect of duty. Further evaluation of all the facts related to the circumstances of the officer's knowledge or actions is necessary."

Aspin said he was not going to transmit this second category of files to the Navy until Dalton was confirmed. "I am holding these files to avoid any perception that current Navy leadership might be either too lenient or too harsh on its fellow members. This should not be seen as a lack of confidence in existing leadership. Rather, it is an attempt to assure all concerned, including uniformed service members and the public, that we have a fair and impartial process for all."

Tailhook '91 occurred in Las Vegas in September 1991. It was the annual convention and symposium of the Tailhook Association, a private organization of past and present naval aviators and others associated with naval aviation. The organization draws its name from the unique feature of naval aircraft, the tailhook that engages arresting wires on carrier decks upon landing.

The first installment of the Inspector General's report on the convention centered on the Navy's response to allegations about conduct at the convention. It was issued September 21, 1992.

-END-

APPENDIX M

NNS817. Secretary of the Navy Releases Tailhook Decision
WASHINGTON (NNS) -- A statement regarding the status of 35 flag and general officers identified by the DoD Inspector General as having been in Las Vegas during the Tailhook '91 convention was released by Secretary of the Navy John H. Dalton today (Oct. 15).
The complete text of SECNAV's statement is as follows:
"I have made some very difficult decisions regarding the status of 35 flag and general officers identified by the DoD IG as having been in Las Vegas during the Tailhook '91 convention. These decisions were not easily reached. I have spent the vast majority of my time in office carefully weighing the facts in an effort to do what is right for the naval service. With the help of the Chief of Naval Operations, Admiral Frank Kelso, the Vice Chief of Naval Operations, Admiral Stan Arthur, the counsel of other senior government officials and with the concurrence of Secretary of Defense Aspin, I have made decisions which I believe deal firmly and fairly with those involved.
It is clear to me that there was a failure of appropriate leadership at Tailhook '91. I strongly believe in the principle of accountability and responsibility. It is the foundation of leadership in the naval service.
The greatest accountability lies with those who were responsible for planning, organizing, and running the convention and those who were responsible for supervising the majority of the active duty members who attended it. For many years, the individual who was responsible for coordinating official Navy support of Tailhook was the Assistant Chief of Naval Operations for Air Warfare. In 1991 this was Vice Admiral Richard Dunleavy More than any other individual, Vice Admiral Dunleavy was responsible for the failures at Tailhook. His performance of duties after Tailhook was similarly flawed.
However, Vice Admiral Dunleavy was not alone in his failure. His active duty and reserve deputies, RADM Riley Mixson and RADM Wilson Flagg, played key roles in the organization and administration of Tailhook '91.
Vice Admiral Dunleavy and these two other officers had an obligation to make themselves aware of the behavior of their juniors in general and persons within their administrative chains of command in particular. They were expected to ensure that such conduct was not unbecoming of naval officers, discreditable to the naval service, or otherwise unacceptable.
There were ample signals that trouble could arise -- precedents of unacceptable conduct at prior Tailhook conventions, visible use of alcohol to excess, resistance and hostility toward women entering what many aviators considered to be a male-only professional domain, and widespread attendance at the event for the sole purpose of having a good time. That potential was heightened by an atmosphere in which rank and the rules of propriety and deference toward rank were set aside for the purposes of Tailhook.
As a result of careful review of the facts, a detailed review of the DoD IG's report and personal interviews with the officers involved, I have determined that no action is warranted concerning two officers and have taken the following actions concerning 33 flag officers:
-- I have issued a Secretarial Letter of Censure to Rear Admiral Dunleavy. Rear Admiral Dunleavy retired from the Navy last summer in the grade of Rear Admiral, one star lower than the highest rank in which he served, which could represent as much as

$100,000 or more during his retirement. I have determined that he will remain on the retired list in the two-star grade of Rear Admiral. This is no minor sanction.
– RADM Mixson and RADM Flagg have also been issued Secretarial Letters of Censure.
In the case of two officers, Major General Clyde Vermilyea and Rear Admiral William Newman, I have concluded that no personal accountability or responsibility for Tailhook is warranted. These officers were present only for an afternoon professional symposium and departed immediately thereafter. They should not be identified with Tailhook in any way.
The remaining 30 officers including Admiral Kelso, will receive administrative action appropriate to them individually. Because these actions are non-punitive, it would be unfair for me to reveal the specific action taken in each instance. However, I can state that I have issued Admiral Kelso a non-punitive Letter of Caution. None of these officers, including Admiral Kelso, personally engaged in any wrongdoing. However, with regard to Tailhook their performance was not all that it could have been.
The naval service has suffered greatly as a result of Tailhook. Some senior officers who were there failed to exercise active leadership and take the necessary actions to prevent behavior that was wrong. Effective leadership requires constant attention and positive action.
From these Tailhook actions, there are important lessons to learn – lessons of leadership, accountability and personal conduct. Those values have been the foundation of our naval service throughout its history. They must guide and sustain us throughout our challenging future.
As troubling as the incidents of Tailhook are, we must not lose sight of the fact that the naval service has made extraordinary strides in emphasizing core values and in providing equal treatment and opportunity for all. Inappropriate conduct will not be tolerated in the Navy. The Navy Department today has one of the finest overall programs of any institution in this country to prevent and correct sexual harassment. Our program has served as a model for government agencies, colleges and universities, major industries and other organizations around the nation.
We are changing our institutional mindset. We are opening new occupational fields to women, while providing stern discipline for those who sexually harass others and caring support for their victims. We are not doing so because of Tailhook, but because it is the right thing to do."
The complete text of SECNAV's statement is also available in an ALNAV released Oct. 15; via the Navy Leadership Policy Bulletin Board in the "Articles" section, as file ART0025; or by electronic mail from NAVNEWS(at)nctamslant.navy.mil.
-USN-

APPENDIX N

DEPARTMENT OF THE NAVY
OFFICE OF THE CHIEF OF NAVAL OPERATIONS
WASHINGTON, DC 20350 2000

IN REPLY REFER TO

26 October 1993

From: Rear Admiral Wilson F. Flagg, USNR,
To: Secretary of the Navy

Subj: REBUTTAL TO LETTER OF CENSURE

Ref: (a) JAGMAN 0114B
(b) SECNAV ltr of 15 Oct 93
(c) BUPERS ltr 1000 PERS-00F of 01 Oct 92

1. Per reference (a), I received a Secretarial Letter of Censure on 15 October 1993, reference (b). I have carefully reviewed reference (b) and submit my rebuttal.

2. Reference (b) was issued pursuant to my attendance at Tailhook '91 as the senior Reserve Flag Officer. The purpose of this letter is to clarify two points:

(a) At no time during Tailhook 91 was there any misconduct on my part, and

(b) I observed no actions that I would construe as misconduct during my attendance.

3. In your letter, the statement that I was aware of misconduct and did nothing to prevent it is not accurate. The inappropriate actions which did occur Saturday night were totally unacceptable by any one's standards. If I had been in attendance I would have taken corrective action to preclude this misconduct, as any Flag Officer would. As you are well aware from my earlier statement, I departed late Friday night. While in attendance I spent a fair amount of time mixing with the junior officers on the third deck with my sister and her husband accompanying me. At no time during this period was she incensed, felt threatened, nor did we observe any misconduct on anyone's part. In her own words "the young people were having a good time."

4. Furthermore, as a matter of record, I was not attached to OPNAV (OP-05) at the time of Tailhook '91 nor did I have a part in the planning. I was assigned to Commander, Naval Air Force Atlantic staff in Norfolk, Virginia. I was asked to participate in the event questions arose at the Air Board concerning Reserve issues.

5. Finally, I was informed that the flag officers in attendance at Tailhook '91 would be allowed to finish their current tours and retire in their present grade held. As a result of the Reserve Continuation Board in March 1992, I was selected to continue and given a retirement date of 01 October 1995, reference (c).

APPENDIX N

Subj: REBUTTAL TO LETTER OF CENSURE

I am confident this date is still valid. Therefore, I accept your letter in an effort to close the door on Tailhook 91 and allow all aviation Flag Officers to get on with the challenge of running Naval Aviation. However, in light of my rebuttal to certain allegations contained in your letter, I respectfully request it be reissued as a non-punitive letter of reprimand.

Very respectfully,

WILSON F. FLAGG
Rear Admiral
U.S. Naval Reserve

CPSIA information can be obtained at www.ICGtesting.com
Printed in the USA
BVOW05*1816310816

R7376700001B/R73767PG460741BVX1B/1/P

9 781633 383029